NEW PREFAB

Architecture

Sergi Costa Duran

Production:
Equipo Loft Publications

Editorial coordinator:
Cristina Paredes Benítez

Editor and Texts:
Sergi Costa Duran

Art director:
Mireia Casanovas Soley

Design:
Conxi Papió

English translation:
Rachel Sarah Burden / Equipo de Edición

Editorial project:
2008 © LOFT Publications
Via Laietana 32, 4° Of. 92
08003 Barcelona, Spain
P +34 932 688 088
F +34 932 687 073
loft@loftpublications.com
www.loftpublications.com

ISBN: 978-84-96936-33-1

Printed in China

NEW PREFAB

Architecture

LOFT

INDEX

PRESENTATION

With international ambition and a vision of the future, "New Prefab" presents fourteen residential and twelve non-residential projects as examples of industrialized and prefabricated construction systems for different purposes — homes, nurseries, cultural installations and commercial buildings. Designs are also featured which have not yet been produced, as well as some that will never take shape, but their unique characters make them worthy of inclusion.

The book highlights projects varying from classical solutions to more experimental proposals, and was compiled with the collaboration of 25 studios on four continents (Europe, America, Australia and Asia). Half the projects are from Europe — principally from Austria and Germany — and several are from the United States, which is logical as they are three of the countries in which the prefabrication industry has been most prolific.

As a prelude to the visual exhibition of the projects, the next few pages contain the contrasting opinions of three specialists: Yasuhiro Yamashita (Atelier Tekuto), who provides an historical vision of the prefabricated market in Japan and in the newly emerging China; Martin Despang (Despang Architekten), who confronts the situation of the modular construction market in his native Europe and in the United States, where he works as a university professor for most of the year; and Luis de Garrido, one of the main voices on ecological architecture in Spain, and a specialist in reinforced concrete prefabrication systems.

PREFABRICATION IN JAPAN AND CHINA

The History of Japanese Housing

There are two major changing points in the history of modern housing in Japan: the Meiji Restoration of 1867 (the change from the Shogun feudal system to the Meiji government's new imperial body) and Japan's defeat in World War II in 1945.

The Condition of Housing in Pre-Meiji Japan

The Tokugawa Ieyasu rule existed for nearly 300 years before the Meiji Restoration in Japan. Because there was no major disturbance during this time, culture blossomed in various aspects.

Edo, the central hub of that era, was a city with a population close to one hundred people at one time. It also excelled in aspects such as water regulation and hygiene, and its system of buying and selling waste materials, such as sewage and ash, was particularly notable. It can be said that these inner city systems of waste management were perfect for its time and, because of the use of these types of recyclable systems, nowadays, Edo could be considered a city that implements the Zero Emissions Research Initiative.

As for the quality of the residences of the upper-classes, samurai and the aristocracy, these were made with the highest quality materials, and were built under assumption that they would be lived in for many years. Housing for the general public in the middle of the city, on the other hand, were very simple and cheap.

In Edo, which was overcrowded with wooden houses, the possibility of a wild fire spreading through the city was of particular concern for the community. During a time when fire fighting equipment was poor, a group of men called "hikeshi-shu" ("fire extinguishers" or "firefighters") were quickly able to extinguish fires at their source and prevent them from spreading. As a result, Edo's construction, dismantlement and reconstruction techniques improved dramatically over a short period of time.

Moreover, the motto "The Fight with Fire is the Flower of Edo" (Kaji to Kenka wa Edo no Hana) was created in honor of the young "hikeshi-shu" men's enthusiasm for dismantling wooden housing. The impetuousness of these firefighters not only inspired many modern-day festivals in Japan, but also left a large number of vacant lots between houses. However, tea houses, which are the birthplace of the art of "cha-dou" (the tea ceremony), are built according to the structure of old buildings in the countryside and are mobile.

The Condition of Housing in Post-World War II Japan

After the Meiji Restoration, Western culture and science flooded into Japan. This is when architecture and brick-work techniques from the West were first implemented to create durable housing made from high-quality and long-lasting materials for the elite of the upper-classes.

After Japan's defeat in World War II, the country faced a period of poverty. At the same time America's economic rationalism was introduced. The Japanese adapted very well to this change into rationalism and incorporated it into their society. Within a miraculously short period of time, they went from a defeat in battle to an accomplished rebirth.

During the war, the city's houses were burned to the ground. The demand for housing increased once again after the baby boom (1947–1950) and at the same time a miraculous economic comeback led to a quickly rising demand for highly durable western-style houses among the general population.

It was at this time that the Daiwa House Industry Company, which started by selling simple frame houses built of iron piping (i.e., "Pipe House"), developed the light-gauge steel structure known as a "Midget House" (1959), which became the origin of present day Japan's prefabricated housing. A new era in home sales was ushered in by the emergence of the department store.

Meanwhile, Sekisui Chemical Company, the plastic makers, mastered the industrialized construction method of plastic production and developed the "Sekisui Heim M1" plastic panels (1971) by adopting the innovative technology of the Unit Construction System.

Both these companies produced houses and developed sales methods. Today, Sekisui builds over 20,000 complete houses per year, while Daiwa produces 110,000 a year, making it into one of the largest companies. Sekisui and Daiwa's success in pioneering production and sales methods for prefabrication houses has given birth to many home building companies in Japan. The percentage of Japan's newly constructed single-family prefabrication homes peaked in 1996 between 18%-12% and has become one of Japan's major large scale productions.

In Japan, with its numerous earthquakes, constructive measures for earthquake resistant structures have been given particular emphasis, and hard and soft enhancements have been developed over the past 15 years. Aside from home builders, who have an eye for improved quality, architecture and construction companies have also begun to adopt pre-cut industrialized housing techniques. In 1996, the percentage of prefabrication houses produced by home builders declined. However, rather than saying that the demand for prefabrication houses has become less, it can be said that because much of Japan's housing uses prefabrication techniques, the value and stability of the prefabrication of general housing is improving.

Prefabrication in China

Up until the Ching Dynasty (1644–1912), various imperial dynasties replaced each other throughout China's long history. Thus, the designs of several places reflect the origin of its respective imperial dynasty. For example, the Imperial Palace of the Ching Dynasty, Gugong, is built in a

Mongolian-style architecture, because of the Manchurian imperial dynasty. The Manchurians were world-renowned equestrians under Genghis Khan. The traditional Manchurian house was called a "yurt" ("gel"), a tent made of felt. However, it is difficult to consider these as the Chinese continent's "mobile housing".

After 1894, when China was invaded by Japan, Japanese imperial and military-style buildings were built. Military barracks were designed to be built as quickly as possible using advanced development technologies, on which the original model of today's Japanese prefabricated houses are based.

Despite China's vast expanse of land, the low cost of materials and labor, the country still does not accept the rational form of "rebuild" and "reuse." However, in recent years, the economic development of Beijing and Shanghai, overcrowding and rising costs of land in the cities have led to an increasing demand for "livable" and high-quality housing. As a result, the supply of stable quality prefabrication techniques has gained importance in China's housing industry and the country is gradually adopting the Japanese techniques of industrial prefabrication housing companies.

The Future of Prefabrication from now

It is a well-known fact that prefabricated single-family houses in post-war Japan were affordable and of good quality. Meanwhile, individual housing designs allowed for the creation of different types of architecture as well the study of various construction methods. These studies have led to a change from the opposition toward prefabrication houses to the export of prefabrication housing techniques and the adoption of prefabrication techniques for individual housing design.

Until now, the development of prefabrication has ensured safety and low cost in the increasingly overcrowded cities. However, over the past five years there has been an attempt at spreading the use of recyclable and environmentally-friendly building materials and equipment for prefabrication.

A number of environmentally-friendly, low-cost and rational houses, apartments and offices have been built in Japan's city centers in recent years. This is not only limited to the sale of simple, unit prefabrication houses, but also includes the conversion of existing offices and apartments.

The use of recyclable aluminum, unit construction and environmentally safe equipment is making progress. However, the testing and implementation of these applications show that safe and affordable prefabrication techniques are labeled as environmentally-friendly and are heading towards a new aspect in prefabrication. Until now, prefabrication has been labeled as uncharacteristic and uncultured, although, surely a technique which can contribute positively to the environment, must be able to take center stage in the world of architecture.

Because of this desire, especially in Japan, I believe that we can once again create a sustainable city like Edo and, possibly, save the earth, which is on the brink of a crisis. That is my desire. Moreover, as the chair holders of the Kyoto Protocol (the elimination of CO_2 and other such greenhouse effects) this is our duty as architects in Japan.

Yasuhiro Yamashita is architect, founder of Atelier Tekuto (Tokyo) and associate professor at the Shibaura Institute of Technology and at the University of Tokyo.
www.tekuto.com

THE NEW PREFABRICATED

The legacy and the future of European and American prefabrication
Construction is an instinctive action, while prefabrication needs more planning. Manufacturing is as old as man. Primitive hunting weapons have been found which are evidence of the first prefabrication strategy, taking the place of manual tools which were constructed spontaneously each time hunger struck. With these improved weapons, man increased his hunting ground and moved into the era of prefabricated architecture. He abandoned his old cave, which was the habitat of the instinctive creature using what the earth provided, and became a forward-thinking nomad, whose accommodation formed part of his hunting strategy. In not using the shelter nature provided, he created ephemeral homes, the primitive fore-runner to prefabricated mobile architecture, which presented a combined action between the physical and the spiritual that has never again been equaled in the prefabrication system.

Where has that first prefabrication system, which to such an extent liberated the so-called civilized western cultures, taken us? The original advances in prefabrication banished the cave, but ironically, as far as the modernist ideals of 'light, air and sun' are concerned, the progress of civilization seems to have returned to it. Having reached the supposed highest point of our evolution, prefabrication — the youngest but most efficient tool of an optimistic modernity — has been degraded to bashfully hidden and masked tight standard frame wood skeletons, resulting in the neo-colonial McMansions which today make up the numerous residential neighborhoods of North America.

The difference between prefabricated homes in North American and in Europe could lie in how near or far both cultures are from their origins. With Fuller's Dymaxion House, Entenza's Case Study Program, Eichler's houses, the contemporary bravery of Dwell Magazine, and a workforce of young, *avant-garde* architects, North America has always been more adventurous than Europe and has fought for its young legacy to avoid returning to the world of the caveman. On the other hand, Europe has used its long history to create a greater diversity in the prefabricated home sector. In society as a whole, however, specifically in terms of following this evolutionary thread, there is a common mistake which is more evident in the field of common architecture, as demonstrated by the numerous factories and warehouses where emphasis has been placed exclusively on efficiency, creating highly negative coldness. The same has happened with housing.

With the beginning of the new century it is possible to see a change in patterns which can be explained by the concept of sustainability. The popular current tandem of sustainability and prefabrication cannot, however, fulfill its promise if we repeat the mistake of being concerned only with the physical. But the premises to start again are attractive: the main strategy of the new

post-fossil prefabrication of the 21st century could be a new impartiality and the humanistic use of technology. So, for now, with ETFE we can make reality of the fleeting dreams of Fuller, following the nomadic tradition of light constructions and through the 'vacuum sealed insulation panels' of the Metabolists; and in the future it will be more so, as some American scientists have already developed bio-degradable plastic without petroleum. Classic construction materials will also be redefined. For example, wood will be reinforced by thermal treatment and, depending on its use as sheets of wood or thick, compact, unclad film which provides healthy climatization, will offer multiple solutions, and will become the new discovery which will change current light wood housing in the United States. The introduction of Phase Changing Materials (PCMs) will also help to solve the lack of thermal storage in light, prefabricated buildings, while at the same time prefabricated cement components will be rediscovered for their durability and thermal properties.

The growing architectural interest in bionics should do more to improve the image of prefabrication and refute the traditional stigma that it is monotonous for being repetitive. Nature is the best example of the fact that a massed collection of similar elements is far from boring; so we place our hopes in the next generation of digital prefabrication. Our idea is that, during the manufacture of mechanized components, and those controlled by computer, the construction architects in front of the computer must be allowed to influence the production in a direct way. The more varied the ideas of the planner, the more varied the products will be. Each finished piece will be unique and in this way the negative image of boring or monotonous prefabrication will be eradicated.

The younger generation must take on the challenges of their century and so re-conquer, in the same strategic way as their ancestors, the discipline of prefabrication as a pragmatic and poetic exercise.

Martin Despang, architect in Hanover, Germany, and Associate Professor at the University of Nebraska in Lincoln, U.S.A. www.despangarchitekten.de

CURRENT SITUATION OF PREFABRICATED CONSTRUCTION IN EUROPE

Origin

Prefabricated construction originally began in an attempt to reduce costs and speed up the construction process. To this end processes of repetition, modularity, integration, normalization and optimization were created, and various strategies were developed for part of the building process to be carried out in factories.

This type of proposal has probably been considered since the beginning of the Industrial Revolution, but the generalized development had to wait until the global reconstruction of cities following the Second World War. At that time a lot of construction was necessary, and had to be done quickly and economically, as there was little money available. This process lasted longer than it should have done, continuing until the high population growth of the years from 1960 to 1970, which was reinforced by the huge migration of people into the cities.

Prefabricated construction extended throughout Europe, although it was particularly intense in the more industrialized and the eastern countries and less evident in the hotter, less industrialized countries, and those with a greater cultural and historical background. As a result, a thriving prefabricated construction industry grew in northern Europe, while in southern Europe it barely progressed.

Possibly the main problem with prefabrication has been that it has not had a chance to evolve sufficiently. It has virtually remained in its initial stages, even though technology now enables the construction of all kinds of high quality buildings at a reasonable price. The fundamental reason for this stagnation has been social rejection.

The reason for this is two-fold. To begin with, the first prefabricated houses built in the old communist countries were small, poor quality and looked like rabbit hutches or barracks, and the aspect of these buildings quickly became associated with the concept of prefabricated homes. Consequently, despite its extensive evolution and the variety of shapes available with current prefabricated construction systems, people still have the same perception of prefabricated buildings.

Secondly, following the fall of communism, eastern countries continued building prefabricated properties. They are, in fact, high quality — some consider them to be the best houses built in the last 5 years — but people associated the concept of prefabricated houses with the shortages of the communist regime and so rejecting the regime implied rejecting prefabricated homes.

Evolution of prefabricated systems and the freedom of design

There are three different stages in the evolution of industrialized and prefabricated construction systems. The first was the development of products with very rigid shape solutions, which seriously limited the architects' creative processes. At this point, architectural solutions centered mainly on the spatial organization of the whole, rather than the design of the houses.

In the second stage, however, products were developed which allowed a certain choice in the designs, and the objective was to create systems of semi-open components. These systems enabled the designers to develop a limited variety of typologies from designs of very elaborate but inflexible components.

We are currently in the third stage. Completely open prefabricated systems are now manufactured which are able to produce a wide variety of possibilities for developing the design of typologies. With current technology and advanced CAD/CAM/CAE systems, it is possible to construct almost any component of a building in the factory, to be assembled later on site.

Prefabrication systems from bases of wood, steel and reinforced concrete

Prefabricated construction in Europe is based fundamentally on the use of three main materials: wood, steel and reinforced concrete. Industrialized construction based on wood has increased considerably in the last decade, due mainly to the elevated cost of houses today. When the average cost of building a residential property in Spain is around 92 Euros/sq. ft., prefabricated wooden construction is barely 56 Euros/sq. ft.

Industrialized and prefabricated construction based on steel modules and frames has had a greater impact in the market, with 12,000 homes a year being built in Spain using steel modules. Without doubt, this fact is due in part to the social perception — which is in fact incorrect — that steel construction is stronger and longer-lasting than wooden buildings. Prefabricated metallic construction is even more extensive in buildings such as schools, hotels, gas stations and administrative spaces in general. The secret of this explosive growth is also due to the fact that this kind of construction can be 30% cheaper than conventional building, and the construction can be carried out in less than a third of the time.

However, the industrialized and prefabricated systems most frequently demanded and employed are based on the use of reinforced concrete, particularly in Spain, which controls almost 10% of the market for concrete in the whole of Europe. Reinforced concrete-based prefabrication offers numerous possibilities which other materials do not. This kind of construction is stronger, more fire-resistant, provides better sound insulation, better thermal inertia, and is more economical and ecological.

The prefabricated concrete industry in Europe is setting the standard in reducing contamination: among others, up to 45% less in the use of traditional materials, 30% less in the use of electrical energy and 40% less in demolition waste. In addition, several concrete recycling plants have been built in the last few years, and future prefabrication factories will function as closed systems, in which everything will be processed, recycled and industrialized to produce new elements for construction.

The future of prefabricated construction in Europe

In the last five years Europe has become an experimental area which frequently stretches habitual concepts to the limit to provide solutions to new construction challenges. Technology has evolved considerably and prefabrication systems currently enable the creation of almost any kind of building. However, despite this rapid progress in technology, society still has a negative perception of prefabricated construction, which makes its development and use more difficult.

So with a view to the future, it is important to spread examples of prefabricated architecture as widely as possible so that society can see it is attractive, functional and comfortable, as well as flexible, sustainable, economic and quick to assemble.

Luis de Garrido is Doctor of Architecture and Computer Science and holds a master's degree in Urbanism. He is president of ANAS, the *Asociación Nacional para la Arquitectura Sostenible* (National Association for Sustainable Architecture) and guest professor at the Massachusetts Institute of Technology (MIT) in the United States. He also directs a master's degree course in Sustainable Architecture, in Valencia, Spain.
www.luisdegarrido.com

WATERSHED

Erin Moore

This studio-workshop is located in the rural community of Benton County in Oregon, close to small farms and the area irrigated by the Marys River, which attracts a large number of birds. The client wanted a studio in which to write in peace and watch the birds. The installation of the structure on the lot was done in such a way as to create as little impact as possible: without building access roads, without electricity and with no excavation of earth.

The floor-space is rectangular; the longitudinal sections correspond to the east and west façades. The structure is made up of three main parts: the reinforced concrete base, a steel structure and wooden cladding. The design of the different parts of the building means they can be constructed in the factory and assembled on site.
The reinforced concrete base supports the weight and enables water to drain along the steel

structure, which was purchased separately and installed on the foundations using a crane. Finally, the wooden cladding was attached to the structure with stainless steel screws. The double-glazed windows are fitted into the wooden shell. There are no joints in the whole structure which cannot be dismantled, meaning that the wooden cladding can be replaced or recycled, piece by piece, if necessary. The same applies to the steel structure.

The polycarbonate roof was designed to create a gentle light inside, and also to emphasize the sound of the rain. As the building is not connected to the electricity network, CO_2 emissions are zero. The structure makes full use of sunlight and the reduced size of the windows ensures cross ventilation.

WATERSHED

Architect: **Erin Moore**
Completion: **2007**
Category: **studio-workshop**
Location: **Wren, Oregon, U.S.A**
Construction materials: **steel, red-cedar wood, polycarbonate, glass**
Cost (prefabrication + transport + installation): **6,300 Euros**
Energy consumed during construction: **19,000 MJ or 3 GJ/m² (concrete foundations, steel structure and cedar wood cladding)**
Construction time: **14 days (prefabrication of steel structure and wooden cladding) + 16 days (transport, foundations and installation of cladding and wooden roof)**
Durability: **depending on material (the concrete base will be the most durable)**
Surface area: **70 sq. ft.**

Photo © Gary Tarleton

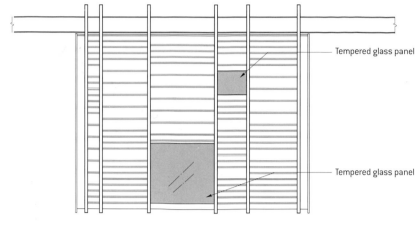

Tempered glass panel

Tempered glass panel

West elevation

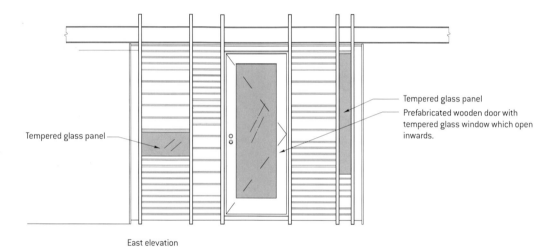

Tempered glass panel

Tempered glass panel

Prefabricated wooden door with tempered glass window which open inwards.

East elevation

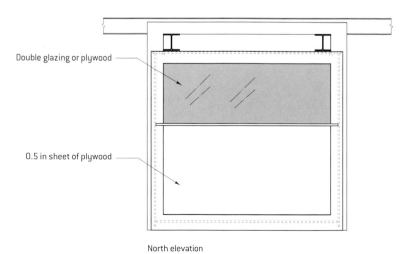

Double glazing or plywood

0.5 in sheet of plywood

North elevation

The client is an author who writes about subjects related to nature and the environment. The building has numerous panoramic openings which enable her to observe the birds and help to inspire her writing.

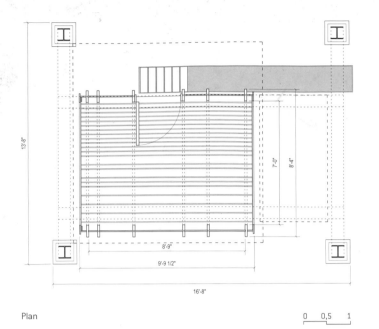

Plan

0   0,5   1

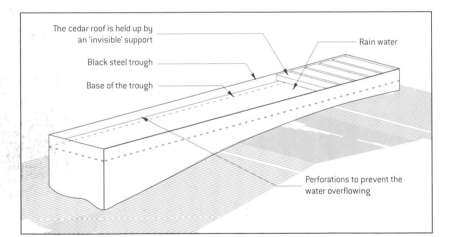

The cedar roof is held up by
an 'invisible' support

Rain water

Black steel trough

Base of the trough

Perforations to prevent the
water overflowing

Trough for collecting water

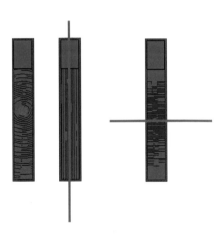

Points where water falls

The roof overhangs all the façades in such a way that it provides
shelter from the rain and shade from the sun. The interior is
simple and the desk occupies the main space.

A longitudinal channel set into the single-pitch roof enables the collection of rain water. This is then stored as a water-trough for the wild-life, although it was also designed to reflect the hydrology of the area, particularly with the sound of falling water.

RUCKSACK HOUSE

Stefan Eberstadt

"The claustrophobic living conditions I experienced in mega-cities like London or New York, when living in small apartments with sometimes only one window towards the outside world, have initiated the idea. Instead of only looking through the window, I imagined the space in front of the window becoming a real new walk-in space." (Stefan Eberstadt in *A-matter* and *Detail*.)

Once constructed on a real scale, Rucksack House was exhibited from September to November 2004 during the international Xtreme Houses exhibition, in Leipzig, Germany, where it was installed for a year. In March 2006 it was also presented in Cologne during the Plan 05 – Forum of Contemporary Architecture symposium.

This project, created by an artist, is between art and architecture, function and shape, private and public property. Rucksack House is a bright space which is a cross between temporary scaffolding and minimalist sculpture. According to the designer, his work tries to address the question of how sculpture can function outside the context of art.

The prototype is a cube shape suspended by steel cables anchored to the roof or façade of the building on which it is a 'parasite'. The inside is completely covered in birch plywood. The fold-away furniture, when opened out, provides shelving, a desk or a bed. The electricity for the space is provided by the building to which it is attached.

RUCKSACK HOUSE

Artist: **Stefan Eberstadt**

Completion: **2004**

Category: **residential extension**

Location: **Leipzig and Cologne, Germany**

Construction materials: **welded steel structure; plywood cladding. Outside: Betoplan (exterior grade plywood with absorbent resin surface), inside: birch veneered plywood; Perspex glazing; steel cables**

Cost (prefabrication + transport): **25,000 Euros (excluding installation)**

Surface area: **96 sq. ft.**

Photo © Frank Motz, Claus Bach, Stefan Eberstadt, Hana Schäfer, Hans-Günter Schäfer, Thomas Taubert, Silke Koch

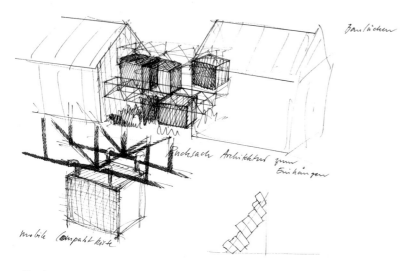

Sketch

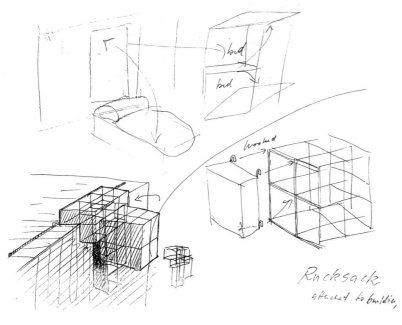

Sketch

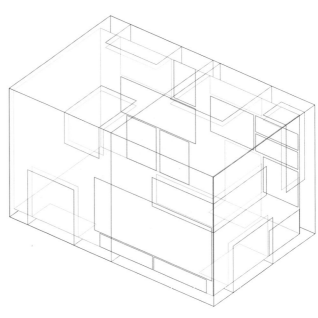

Axonometric view

The cube weighs approximately 1,100 kg. The lineal style of the interior, when the furniture is folded away, is only interrupted by the windows.

The furniture inside folds away, and when the surfaces are opened out they take on different shapes, such as a platform to lie on, a table or a stool. The walls of the prototype, which was initially intended for a temporary exhibition, do not provide insulation, so would need to be adapted if the unit were to be manufactured.

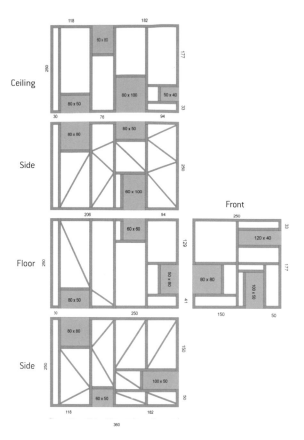

The dimensions of the unit are 8.2 x 8.2 x 11.81 ft. The construction materials are economic and accessible. Stefan Eberstadt chose materials with which he was used to working as an artist.

Measurements of the different parts which make up the prototype

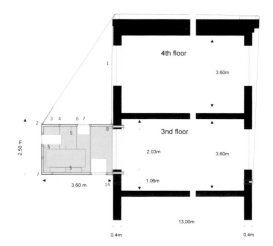

Rear anchoring with steel cable section

1. 0.63 in stainless-steel cable with turnbuckle
2. steel angle with eye, welded to steel frame
3. 0.71 in resin-coated laminated construction board
4. 3.15 x 3.15 x 0.13 in steel SHS cage
5. 0.47 x 0.71 x 0.83 in laminated birch construction board
6. 0.16 in steel flat support for glazing
7. 0.31 in extruded-Perspex fixed glazing, bend to 90° angle at edge of structure, sealed with silicone
8. 9.84 x 9.84 x 0.79 in steel plate welded to steel cage

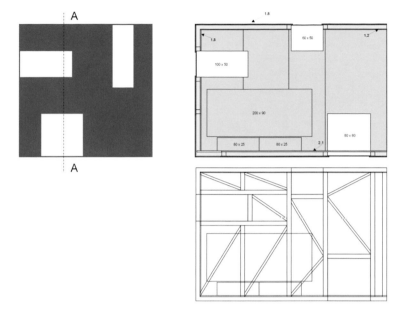

Section A-A

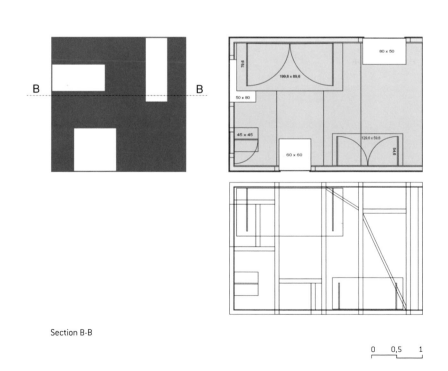

Section B-B

0   0,5   1

1) Can you describe your design strategy?
Space matters! Developing new spatial models is a major concern for me, since we are losing unregulated space in many urban centers at a high rate. As an artist I am constantly experimenting with and redefining space, in particular in-between gaps and unused niches, in order to push its physical properties, social functions, and intellectual boundaries.

2) Do you expect anyone to own one of these structures? Could it be a model for living?
Yes, in some progressive way it reflects the owner's personality. If you're ready for change, the Rucksack House is an ideal statement to express it. Furthermore, it is a perfect example for a piece of art in public space and a great extra space ready for instant use. In an ideal world it certainly could be a model for living.

3) Why do you think that the reaction to the house has been positive?
Probably because the Rucksack House is a direct visual sign and reactivates the idea of the self-built anarchistic tree house, this time however, more prominently placed and structurally engineered. New space gets slung onto an existing space by a simple, clear, and understandable method.

4) If you could choose any building in the world to attach your Rucksack House to which would it be?
I imagine it would be a great model for cities like Tokyo.

Source: the first two questions are extracts from an interview published by the digital magazine 'A-matter' and the technical magazine 'Detail'. The third and fourth questions come from an interview with Albert J. Hill in 'Wallpaper*', London 2005.

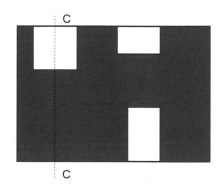

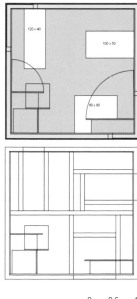

Section C-C

0   0,5   1

The cube allows the transition between two environments: it is a private area which 'floats' in a public one. It also offers extra space to improve quality of life by increasing the habitable area of an existing property.

Philippe Barriere Collective

MTGH is the abbreviation Philippe Barriere Collective uses for its modular structure properties. These prototypes, which are yet to be mass produced, can serve as refuges in emergency situations or for migratory movement. They can also be used as homes if three storeys are combined to form duplexes or triplexes.

The original prototype was designed for a medical investigation center in Sri Lanka, and as a community center in Maai Miau (Kenya). Partly constructed from recycled materials, each model can be dismantled and used with, or in, other MTGH structures. The assembly of two modules creates a frontal façade with a vault-shaped roof, which also ensures the transparency of the façade and the possibility of increasing the height of the structure.

The building is designed to be supported by pillars. The basic modules comprise rectangular floors measuring 387 and 538 sq. ft. respectively. The front façade is completely glazed with glass panels, 2.95 ft wide and 6.99 ft high. The joins are anodized aluminum frames. The sides are made of sheets of corrugated Galvalume (zinc and aluminum) measuring 7.87 ft. The basic model comes with a 5.97 ft wide pivoting glass door. The base of the flooring is light cement on top of galvanized steel sheets. The curved roof is made from a plank of wood measuring 3.94 ft, 'floating' in relation to the structure of the roof. For the duplexes and triplexes the sides have slatted shutters. The MTGH modules have a bio-climatic design with 13.12 ft high ceilings, which enable cross ventilation.

MTGH

Architect: **Philippe Barriere Collective**

Completion: **prototype**

Category: **residential**

Construction materials: **wood (roof), aluminum (walls, ceiling), glass (front façade)**

Cost (prefabrication): **a) 538 sq. ft. unit: Structural frame and lot: 25,328 Euros**

Walls (3.97 ft section): **6,407 Euros. Roof (3.97 ft section): 1,106 Euros**

b) **387 sq. ft. unit: Structural frame and lot: 19,144 Euros. Walls (3.97 ft section): 5,825 Euros**

Roof (3.97 ft section): **922 Euros**

Glazed façade and covering for interior walls (depending on size and type): **5.20 Euros/sq. ft.**

Construction time (prefabrication + installation): **3 days (modules measuring 538 sq. ft. and 387 sq. ft.)**

Surface area: **basic modules measuring 538 sq. ft. and 387 sq. ft.**

Renderings © Philippe Barriere Collective

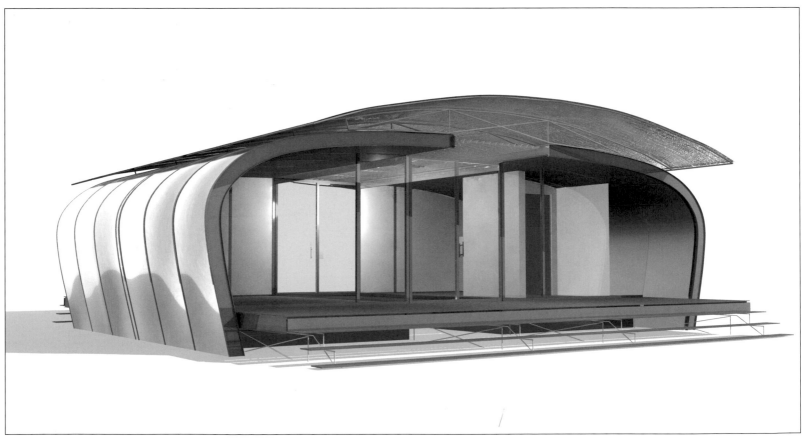

The MTGH modules are prepared to be installed wherever they are needed, principally as shelters for people in transit. The combination of different modules can create residential complexes for limited numbers of people.

1. Pivot door
2. Bathroom
3. Closet
4. Kitchen with fold-out table
5. Open Bay: courtyard / garden
6. Canopy
7. Kitchen
8. Bedroom
9. Master bedroom
10. Sliding door

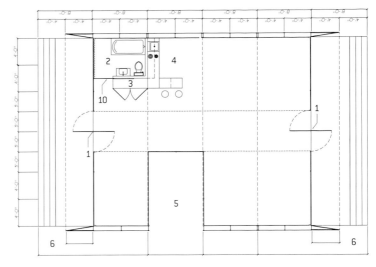

Plan of basic model - Option 1

The basic models can be sold with or without a 'floating' roof. The main access to the property is a double pivoting door.

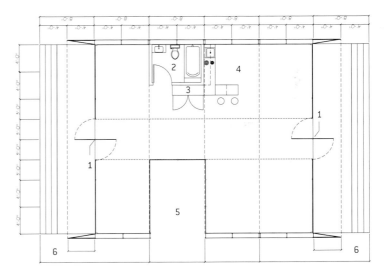

Plan of basic model - Option 2

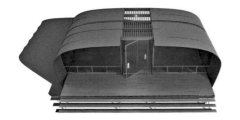

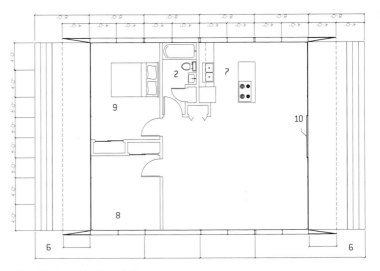

Plan of basic model with two bedrooms

0 1 2

Materials used:

Recycled metal (A. Zahner)

Recycled concrete (Oxford Recycling)

Polygal panels

Roof and external drapes (Powell & Powell Supply Company)

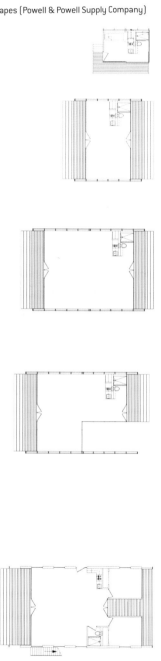

Possible combinations of modules (plans,
elevations and views in perspective).

three modules on top of each other creates a
independent lower module with a duplex
above that has a terrace, two bathrooms and
more than one bedroom.

MTGH duplex:

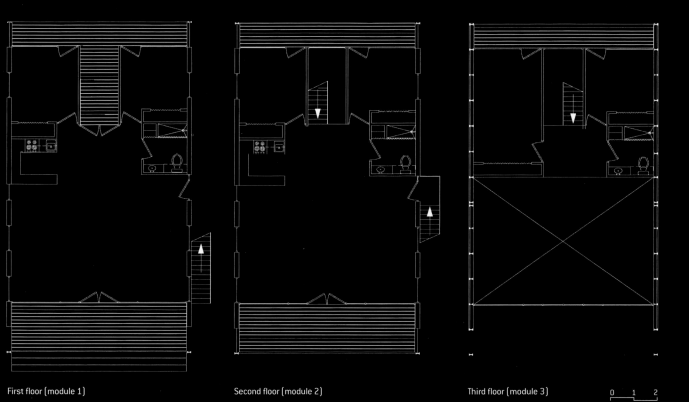

First floor (module 1)

Second floor (module 2)

Third floor (module 3)

0 1 2

EVOLUTIV HOUSE

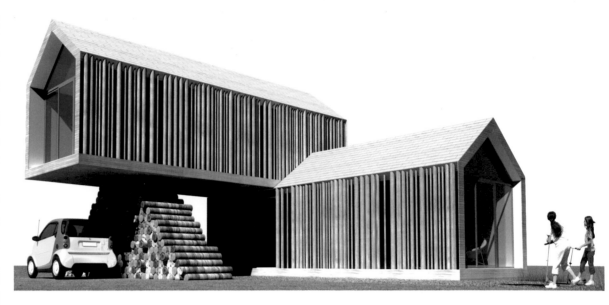

Olgga Architects

This prototype was originally installed at the Alpexpo Grenoble Fair. The architect's initial objective was to construct a low-budget home made of two prefabricated modules which could be combined in different ways to create different styles. The way both structures pivot can also vary, either by using a pile of trunks to support the upper storey or by placing the two units on top of each other in the same direction. Either option creates a wide variety of exterior spaces. In terms of marketing, the client can choose the number of modules they want to combine and the support system to be used. Another option offered is a garden area on the roof at the top of the building.

The standard height of each module is 18.37 ft. The basic module has a living area with dining room and an integral kitchen in one space, and also includes a bathroom with shower at one end. Next to this is the staircase, leading to a second floor with a single and a double bedroom, as well as a bathroom with a bath-tub. The energy used during the construction of this property is 48 kWh/m²/year. Other environmentally-friendly advantages of this prototype are its low energy consumption (it uses thermal solar panels located on the roof), its flexibility and the use of natural materials such as chestnut wood and thermal insulation from a base of wood shavings. If requested, the model also offers the option of collecting rain water to be used in the bathrooms and to water the garden.

EVOLUTIV HOUSE

Architect: **Olgga Architects**
Completion: **2008**
Category: **residential**
Location: **Alpexpo, Grenoble, France**
Construction materials: **chestnut wood**
Cost (prefabrication + transport + installation): **100,000 Euros (before taxes)**
Construction time: **1 month (prefabrication) + 2 days (installation)**
Durability: **decades**
Surface area: **753 sq. ft.**

Photo © Patrick Blanc, Pauline Turmel

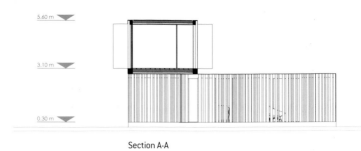

Section A-A

Longitudinal elevation

Section B-B

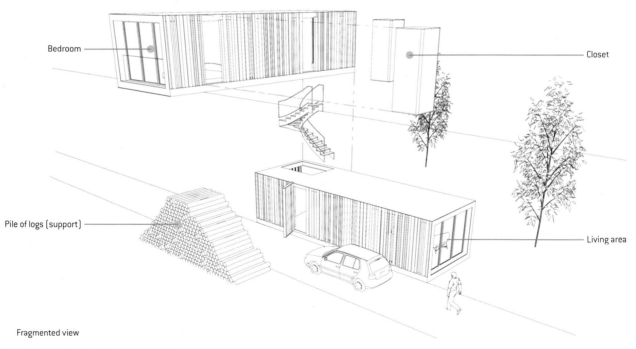

Bedroom

Closet

Pile of logs (support)

Living area

Fragmented view

The original model comprises two bodies shaped like shipping containers, located perpendicularly, with one end of the upper part being supported by a pile of wooden logs stacked like a pyramid.

The model was exhibited at the European Wood Fair (www.salondubois.com), held in Grenoble each April at the Biennale of Sustainable Habitat. A similar model has been constructed in the forest on the outskirts of the city.

Another possible combination is to put two units on top of each other, resulting in a double-storey property with a rectangular floor-space, similar to the prefabricated construction plan with shipping containers.

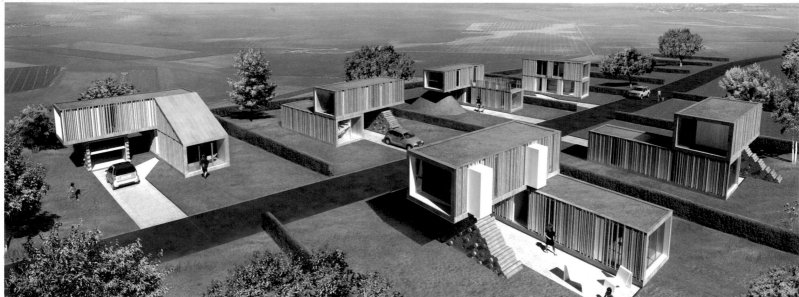

The original prototype was clad in chestnut wood. The possibility to create an eco-community made up of prefabricated modules is another option for the future.

First floor

Second floor

0 1 2

2

5

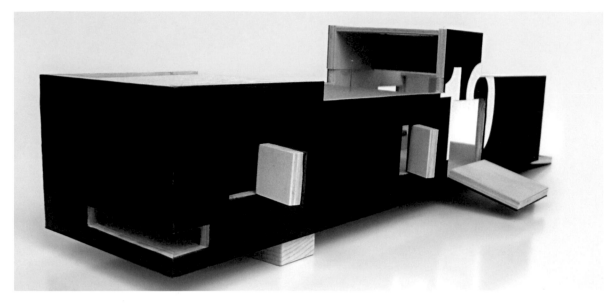

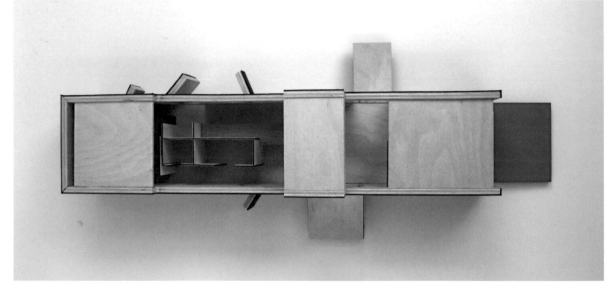

Korteknie Stuhlmacher Architecten, Bikvanderpol

This project was subsidized by the SEV within their IFD program. SEV refers to The Steering Committee for Experiments in Public Housing, an autonomous organization which provides economic support for initiatives related to construction in Holland. House Nº 19 is located in Leidsche Rijn, a new residential neighborhood to the west of Utrecht. This zone serves as an exhibition area and a meeting point for students of the Dutch Art Academy. The concept for the project came from the artists' need for a work space when they are traveling or when they have moved away from home. This model, 100% prefabricated, meets the needs of residents in transit.

The space, which can also be a home, can be used as a hotel room, a studio or simply as a meeting place.

The floor-space is rectangular, and one end can be opened to create a ramp, or converted into a type of exterior deck. The elevation is irregular: close to the central part of the premises there is an elevated section which increases the covered living space. The flooring, the walls and the ceiling have a structure of soft wood sheets put together with steel frames. The load-bearing wooden walls are covered with water-resistant, thermal insulation.

HOUSE Nº 19

Architect: **Korteknie Stuhlmacher Architecten, Bikvanderpol**
Completion: **2003**
Category: **studio-workshop, residential**
Location: **Utrecht, Netherlands**
Materials: **wood, steel**
Construction time: **1 week**
Durability: **decades**
Total constructed surface: **775 sq. ft.**

Photo © Christian Kahl, Korteknie Stuhlmacher Architecten

40. Studio-workshop. **Korteknie Stuhlmacher Architecten, Bikvanderpol**

The design is based on the shape of a shipping container. At one end the gates can be opened to serve as a ramp or a deck. The dimensions of the whole unit are 59.06 x 13.12 x 10.5 ft.

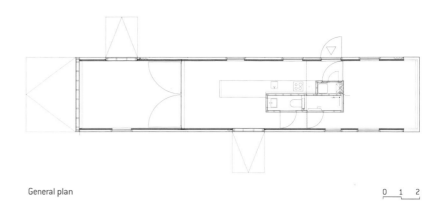

General plan

0 1 2

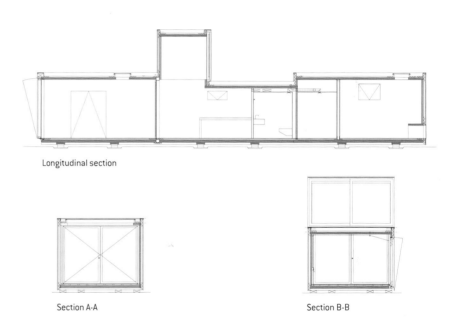

Longitudinal section

There are two exits in the sides, which also open like gates. The other openings are large, wooden windows fitted into the building.

Section A-A

Section B-B

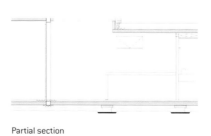

Partial section

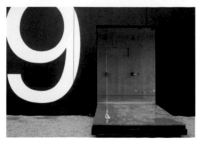

The model does not require bases or
additional structure. Being a compact unit,
it can be moved from one place to another
using just one crane.

This prototype is the result of the efforts of two teams specialized in architecture for mobile situations. Since 2000 the Bikvanderpol duo have formed part of the organization committee for the annual meeting of Nomads and Residents. Likewise, in 1999 the architects Mechthild Stuhlmacher and Rien Korteknie created the Parasite Foundation, an institution dedicated to temporary architectural initiatives.

HOUSE ON ESSEX STREET

Andrew Maynard Architects

Andrew Maynard Architects specialize in creating mobile, flexible spaces, particularly for residential properties. Located in a north Melbourne suburb, this project was to extend a weatherboard house. The client asked for an annex with two bathrooms, a kitchen, a living area and a bedroom, and requested it should be more accessible to the exterior than the existing structure.

The new space was developed on the east-west axis and comprises a wooden structure put together using pieces of recycled steel measuring 0.47 in. The design enables more sunlight to flow into the building. The original house has also been renovated, resulting in a rectangular floor space with four rooms. In terms of distribution, the kitchen and the bedroom form the joining points between the original house and the extension. Andrew Maynard Architects decided to use mobile division walls, inspired by the technology used for mobile telephones, portable lap-tops and PDA. Folding garage doors have been used to close the building. For the bio-climatic aspect, the orientation of the house and other design factors ensure the property is eco-efficient, minimizing the glare of the sun during the summer and maximizing its effects in winter. The structure of the extension has a second skin made of sheets of Western Red cedar wood. There are plans to install a tank on the south façade to collect water, and to put solar panels on the roof.

HOUSE ON ESSEX STREET

Architect: **Andrew Maynard Architects**
Completion: **2005**
Category: **residential extension**
Location: **Brunswick, Australia**
Construction materials: **cedar wood, recycled steel, glass**
Construction time: **8 months**

Photo © Peter Bennetts, Dan Mahon

Located in a suburban area, the use of natural materials (wood),
bright colors and folding doors as screens, give touches of Japanese
interior design to the construction.

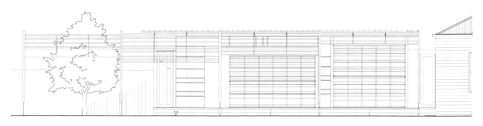

North elevation

The principal ecological measures are the bio-climatic design,
which enables benefit to be made of the sun and of cross
ventilation, and the use of recycled materials in the wooden
structure.

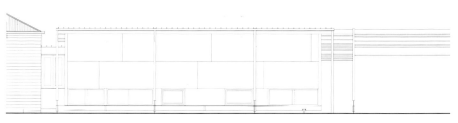

South elevation

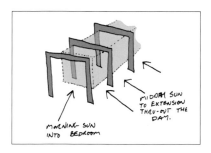

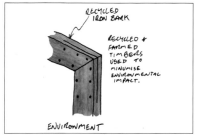

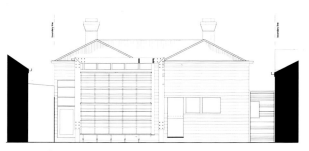

East elevation

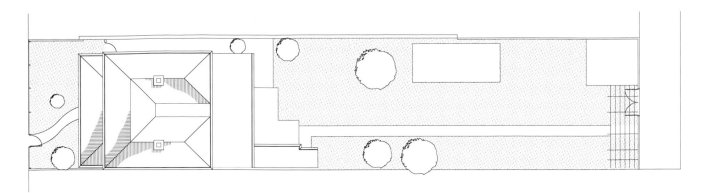

Plan of existing roofs

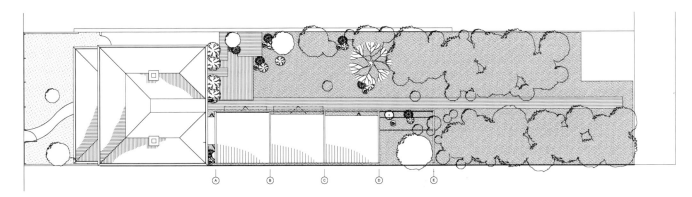

Plan of proposed roofs

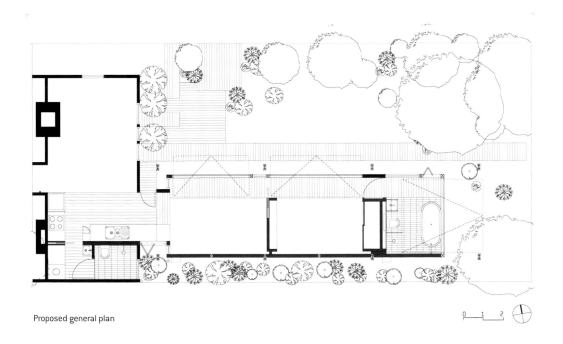

Proposed general plan

0   1   2

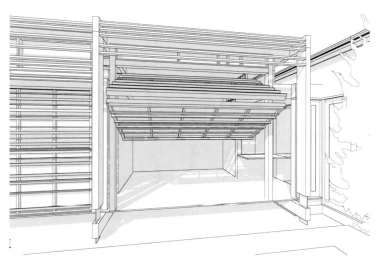

Views of the exterior in perspective

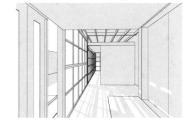

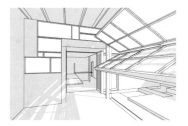

View of the interior in perspective

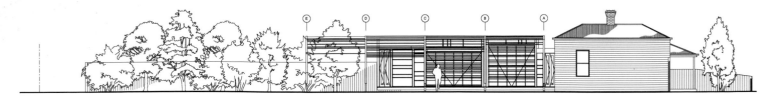

Longitudinal elevation with sections

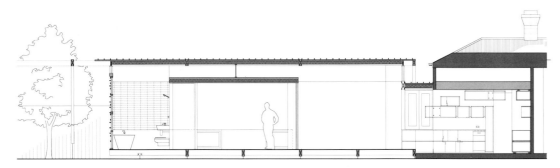

North longitudinal section

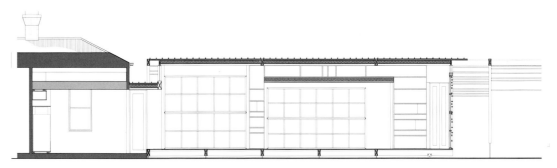

South longitudinal section

The space has been arranged so that one of the bathrooms is located at the farthest end of the original building. The new construction has glazed façades and a double skin of cedar wood shutters.

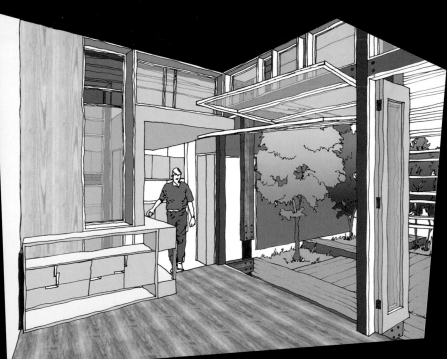

Jeremy Edmiston, Douglas Gauthier/ System Architects

This unique house is located in a cul-de-sac in the suburb of North Haven, an Australian town just five minutes' walk from the beach. It is situated on a lot, measuring 2,378.61 sq. ft., which is more than 100 years old. Local law means the house must be placed on pillars, nearly 6.56 ft off the floor.

The client is a family with three children and two dogs. The design includes three bedrooms, a bathroom, a restroom, a carport for two cars, an open-plan space for the living room, the children's area, the dining room and the kitchen, plus a cricket pitch and a basketball court. Work began in January 2005 and was completed in December of the same year, with the majority of the prefabricated elements already assembled by March.

The geometry of the construction is marked by two sections; each one, located at opposite angles, provokes the reinterpretation of the plan for the interior and exterior of the house. Consequently, in the dining room, light reflects in two directions while, in the living room, light pivots around a point in the roof. When these two visual references come together along the longitudinal axis of the house, the combination offers an infinite collection of changing sections. For this reason, the perception of the constructed area is mutant and affects the design as well as the bio-climatization of the property.

During the year the house only uses passive systems for air-conditioning – bearing in mind the climate in this area is mild. Each section adapts to the sea breezes and the heat of the sun. In summer, the fact that the property is elevated off the ground allows cool air to flow underneath the house.

BURST*003

Architect: **Jeremy Edmiston, Douglas Gauthier/System Architects**
Completion: **2005**
Category: **residential**
Location: **North Haven, Australia**
Construction materials: **concrete, plywood, cedar wood, steel, glass**
Cost (prefabrication + transport + installation): **1,532 Euros/m²**
Construction time: **12 months**
Surface area: **1,001 sq. ft. (house), 495 sq. ft. (deck)**

Photo © Floto + Warner

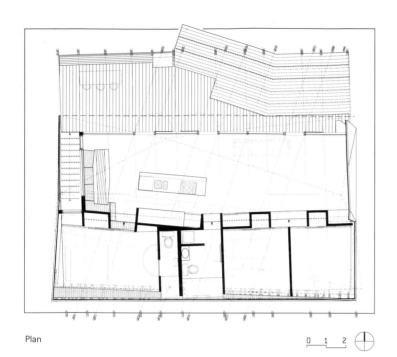

Plan

0 1 2

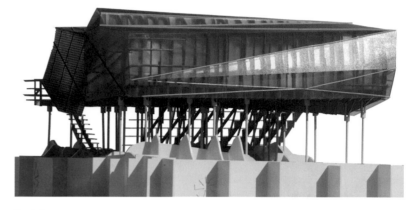

Rendering

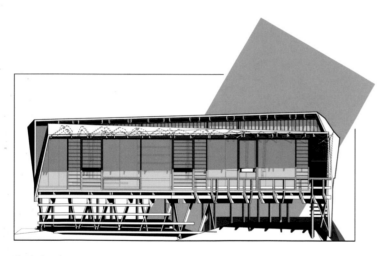

North elevation

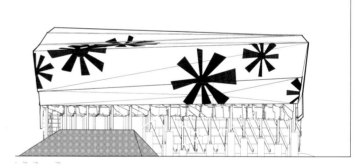

South elevation

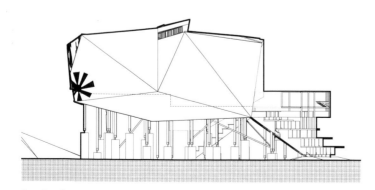

East elevation

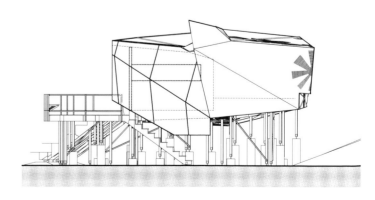

West elevation

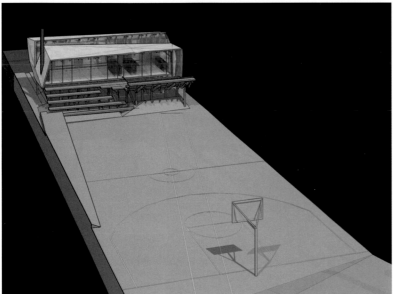

View in perspective from the north

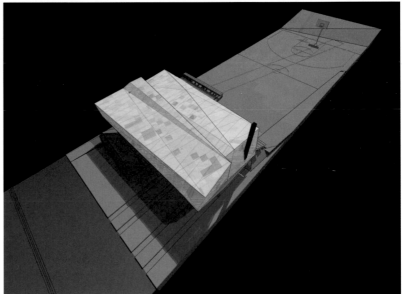

View in perspective from the south

Burst*003 is an alternative to massive production models; it provides varied, multiple solutions to expand geometries and shapes, and offers housing with a guarantee.

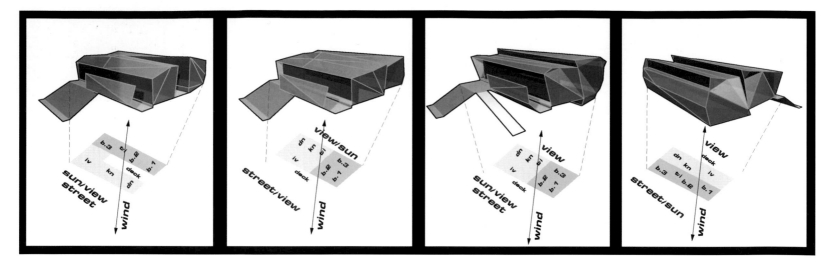

Bio-climatic diagram depending on orientation

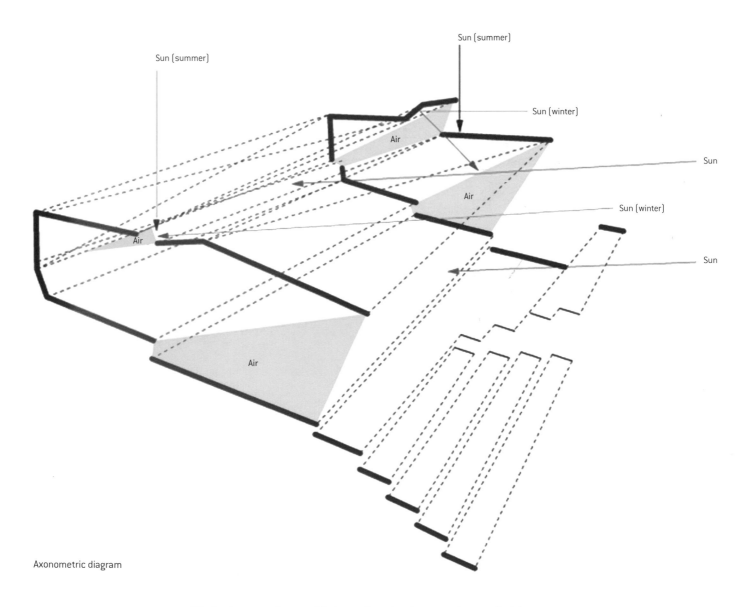

Axonometric diagram

Rendering of dining room

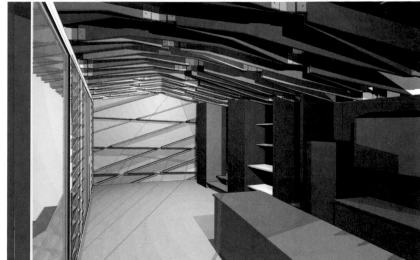
Rendering of living room

Rendering of inside towards exterior deck

Rendering of parking area

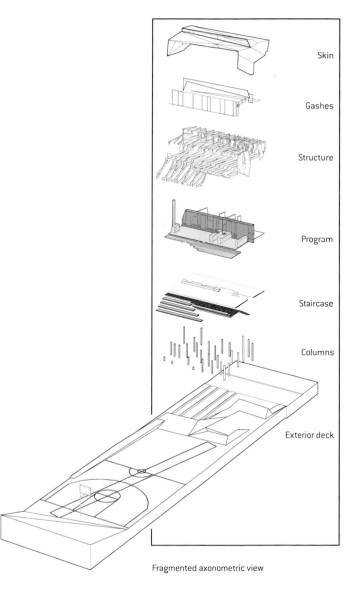

Skin

Gashes

Structure

Program

Staircase

Columns

Exterior deck

Fragmented axonometric view

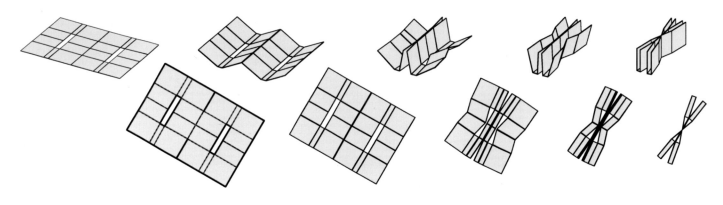

Axonometria of ribs and joints

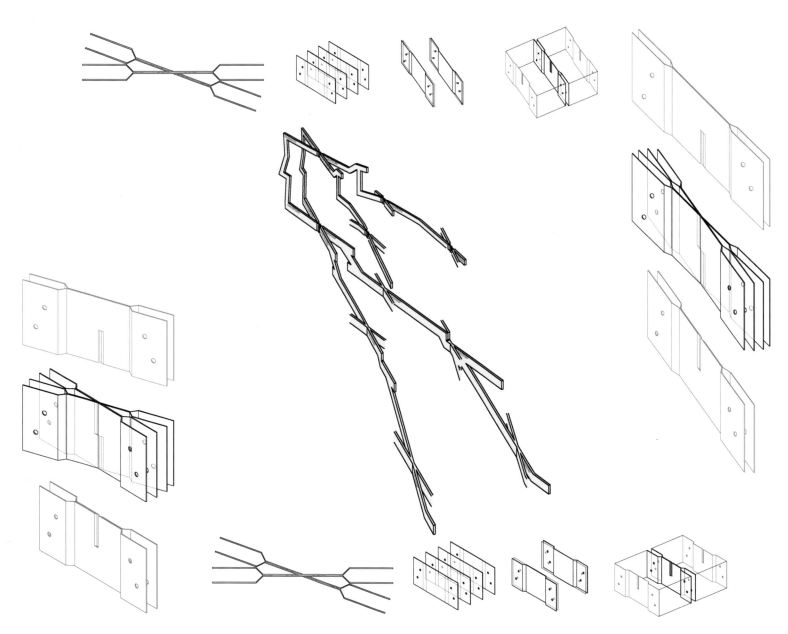

Axonometria of the folds of the ribs

The construction system includes a plywood rib structure, 0.98 in wide and cut using a laser. Each rib has previously been numbered and cut according to its position. The floor is completed with two layers of 0.47 in plywood with a resin finish.

The concept:

This house is receptive to flexibility and changes in structural, design and environmental parameters. If its use changes, the property can be extended or reduced as needed.
Burst prototypes can be found on the east coast of Australia. It is a kind of house in which each element is pre-cut and numbered at the factory, transported to the site and assembled there. Using digital design processes, a complex geometry can be created, adapted to the relation between natural forces in the area and the design. This creates a house with low energy consumption which uses construction materials in an intense and very efficient way.
For these prototypes, System Architects have developed patented overlays which standardize the construction, as well as its adaptability to environmental, structural and design parameters. This means that one type of building can be ideal in different climates, locations and programs, and will be able to withstand earthquakes, hurricanes and floods. Through a series of deliberate overlaps, gaps and slits within the building's skin, one's eye obliquely captures the surrounding landscape to interiorize the exterior. The human figure moves within, over and under the folded skin, ambiguously occupying inside and outside.

In summer, the dining room, kitchen and living room are protected from the sun by the roof. The use of glazed wall-curtains with steel door-frames enables views of the exterior throughout the year. The bedrooms, which are off the living room, are completely interior. Grilles in the walls enable cross ventilation.

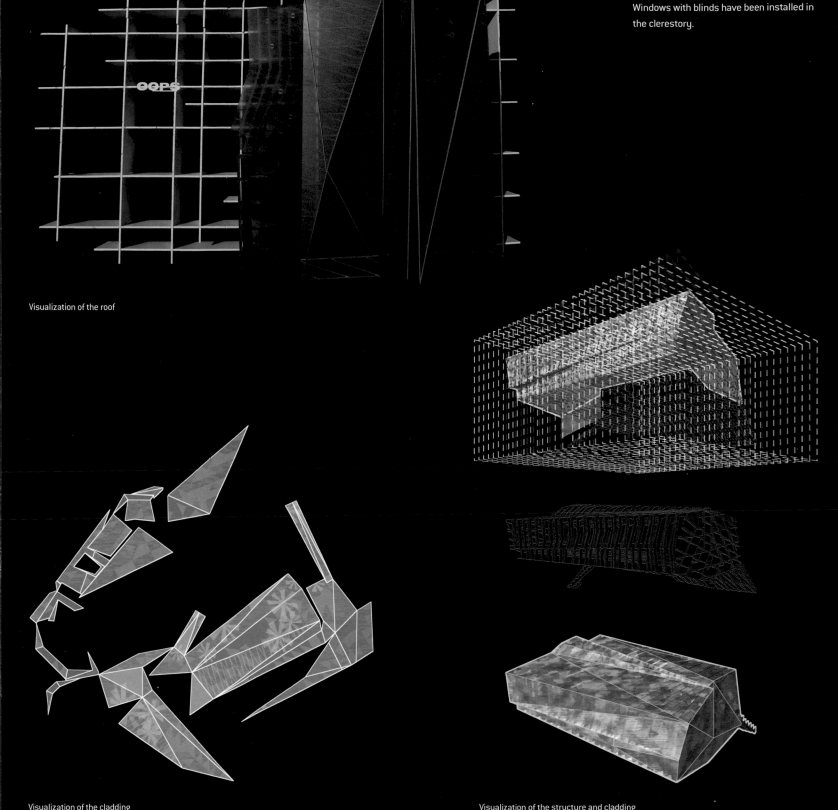

OOPS

Windows with blinds have been installed in the clerestory.

Visualization of the roof

Visualization of the cladding

Visualization of the structure and cladding

HOUSE OF STEEL AND WOOD

Ecosistema Urbano Arquitectos

Located in rural surroundings in Asturias, Spain, this house is a contemporary reinterpretation of models of traditional architecture (like a *hórreo* – a wooden granary raised on pillars, typical in Asturias - with glazed gallery, using wood in the structure and walls). The building is anchored to the ground in just four places, so respecting the site and creating a compact effect. The unit is formed by a prism which is irregular on the south-west side, allowing more sunlight to flow inside. The roof slopes towards the hillside, enabling rainwater to run off easily. The south façade is completely glazed.

The mixed structure of the building, made from steel and wood, can be dismantled and recycled. The walls are made from a combination of two types of wood (North Pine and Douglas Pine) in different widths.

The architects consider the building to be flexible, transformable and suitable for sharing. Its position and geometry adapt perfectly to the climate and solar orientation of the area. The property does not have heating or air-conditioning installations.

HOUSE OF STEEL AND WOOD

Architect: **Ecosistema Urbano Arquitectos**
Completion: **2005**
Category: **residential**
Location: **Ranón, Asturias, Spain**
Construction materials: **steel and wood**
Cost (prefabricated): **150,000 Euros**
Durability: **50 years**
Surface area: **969 sq. ft.**

Photo © Emilio P. Doiztua

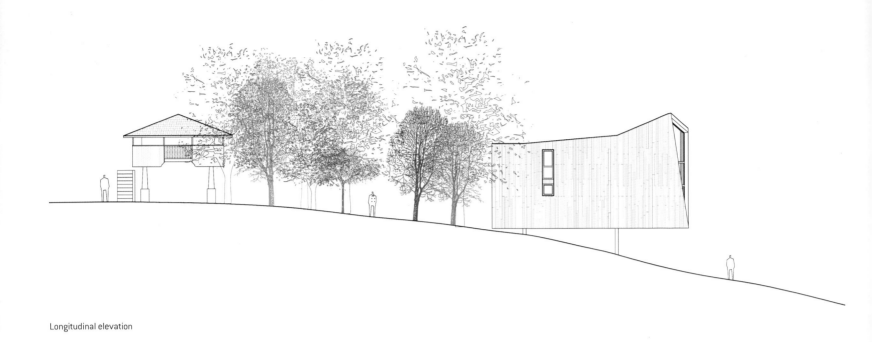

Longitudinal elevation

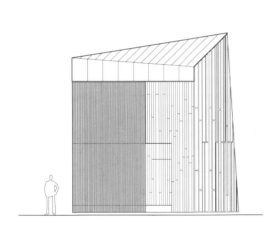

Transversal elevation

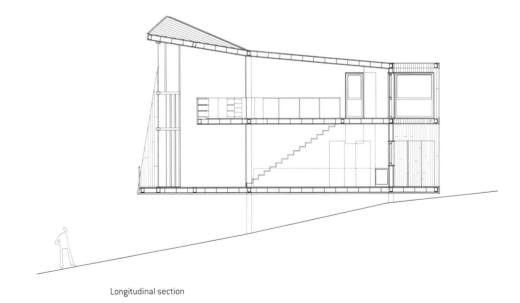

Longitudinal section

Bio-climatization is assured by façades which are almost totally covered, avoiding th ermal losses. Air can flow in and out of all the façades, creating cross ventilation inside the house.

The north façade is protected by means of an anterior space and wind-blocking lattice window. The double-storey height was not created with spatial or composite ends, but is a bio-climatic device fundamental for the thermological functioning of the house.

Surface gaps N = 91 sq. ft.
Surface gaps W = 22 sq. ft.
Surface gaps E = 63 sq. ft.
Surface gaps S = 448 sq. ft.

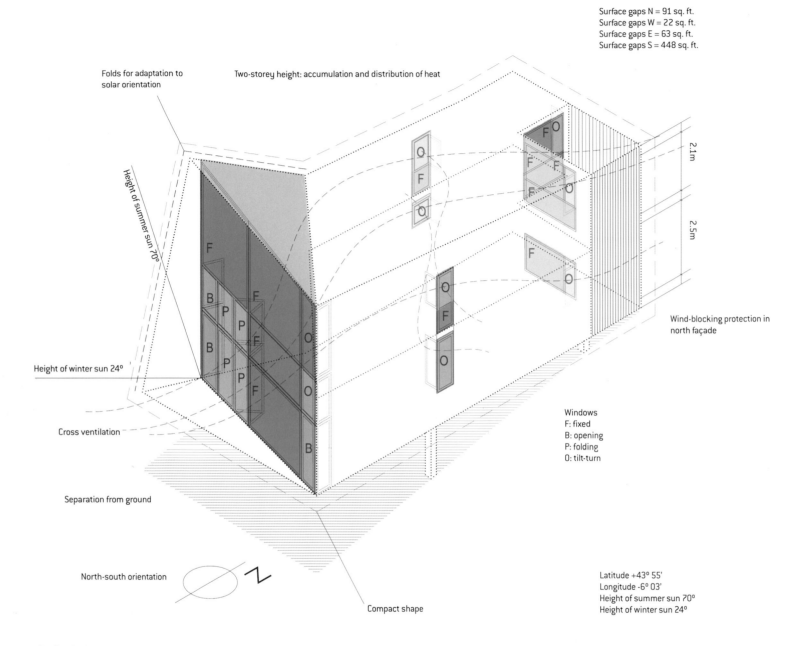

Folds for adaptation to solar orientation

Two-storey height: accumulation and distribution of heat

Height of summer sun 70°

2.1 m

2.5 m

Height of winter sun 24°

Cross ventilation

Wind-blocking protection in north façade

Separation from ground

Windows
F: fixed
B: opening
P: folding
O: tilt-turn

North-south orientation

N

Compact shape

Latitude +43° 55'
Longitude -6° 03'
Height of summer sun 70°
Height of winter sun 24°

Bio-climatic diagram

The combination of laminated steel profiles creates a prism which twists the south façade. The position of the property on a sloping lot makes the façade a look-out point over the Asturian countryside.

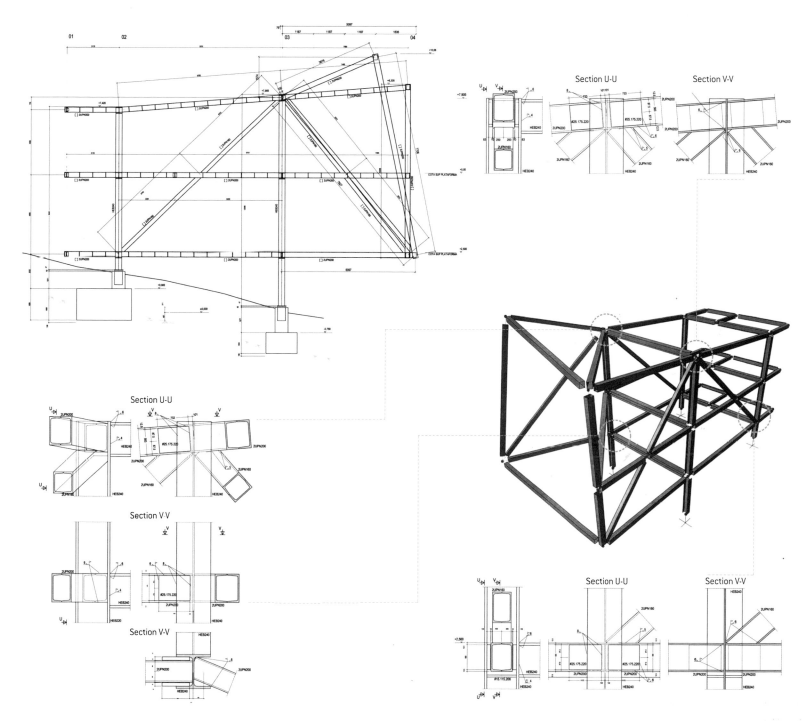

Structure in detail

East façade

North façade

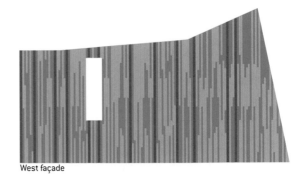

West façade

Lower wall

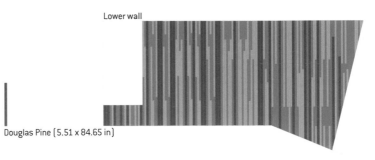

Detail of wooden wall

North Pine (3.54 x 129.92 in)

Douglas Pine (3.54 x 84.65 in)

Douglas Pine (5.51 x 84.65 in)

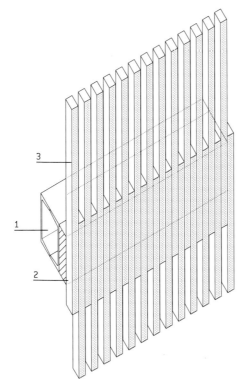

3

1

2

1- Main structure. Profiles of laminated steel 2UPN200, in pairs, creating drawer. Epoxidic imprimation of 60 μm. Finished layer 40 μm.

2. Wooden sleeper. 204.72 in North Pine. Weather treated. Attached to the main metal structure with screws.

3. Wooden shutter. 1.20 in separation 1.18 in. Screwed to wooden sleeper.

Detail of shuttered wall

Instead of a conventional system of adjustable slats, Ecosistema Urbano Arquitectos created shade from the sun using a system of gaps in different positions and combinations, which act like a higrothermic regulator and provide a more suitable solution for the microclimate in the area.

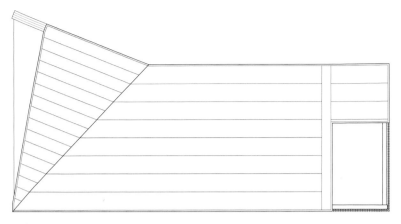

Roof

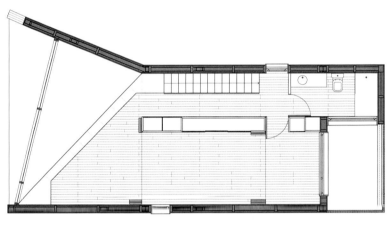

Second floor

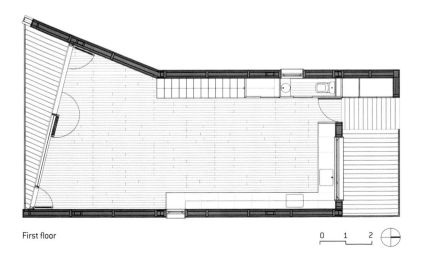

First floor

0   1   2

"The *hórreo* is a construction which provides a solution to the problem created by the extreme dampness which is typical of the climate and the soil in Cantabria, and the need for dry conditions in warehouses storing cereals or its products, in order to prevent them rotting. The *hórreo* is therefore a primitive bio-climatic mechanism, like many others which exist in rural surroundings." (Miguel Martínez Garrido)

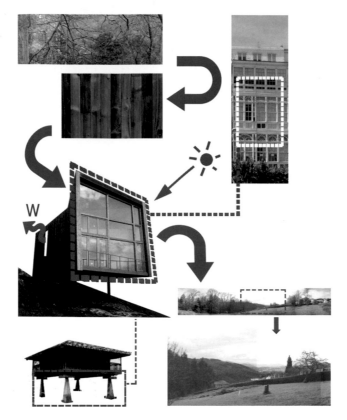

Ideogram

The exterior cladding is made of 1.38 in tongue and groove board. Inside, the wooden flooring and the covering on the ceilings are also made from the same material.

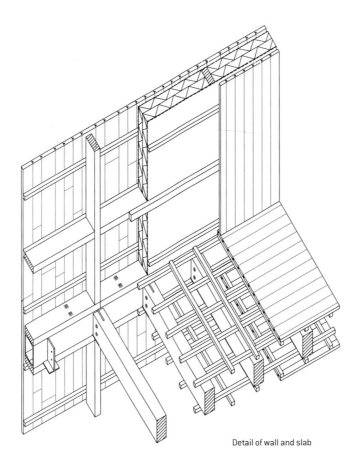

Detail of wall and slab

The first floor incorporates different uses in one space, which can be arranged by the residents in various ways; the second floor can comprise between one and three bedrooms.

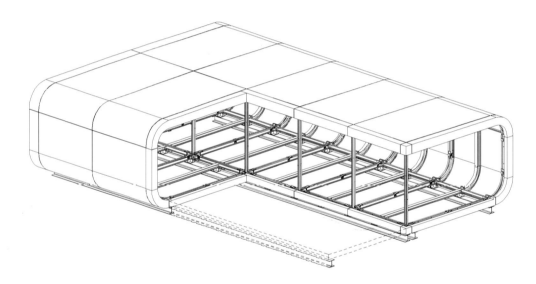

Hobby A. Schuster & Maul, Gerold Peham

Nomadhome is a patented system of flexible construction which consists of joining 118 sq. ft. modules, that can then be used commercially or for housing. The modules can be interchanged, extended or dismantled at any time. The structure can be taken down in two or three days and the modules can be transported by road.

The design, by Gerold Peham, aims to provide totally flexible housing as a symbol of life in the 21st century. The modules are purchased, but can be assembled on a rented lot. According to Gerold Peham, the construction also has a temporary and independent character.

The use of sandwich panels for the structure, and an installation system which can easily be adapted to all modules, means that an unlimited number of modules can be added to an individual unit. They are transported by road and installed on site.

The basic house is made up of approximately 538 sq. ft. which end up looking like 753 sq. ft. thanks to Gerold Peham's ability to distribute the interior spaces without using dividing walls, in the style of an industrial loft. The external cladding can be different materials, as preferred: aluminum, copper, corrugated steel, larch wood and sheets of PVC in the color of choice. The colors inside can also be altered as requested.

The electrical, automated and heating / air-conditioning systems are modular and extendable, given the connection system used. According to the European regulations for energy efficiency in houses, the building is classified with the letter C: its consumption is 62.7 kWh/m^2.

NOMADHOME

Architect: **Hobby A. Schuster & Maul, Gerold Peham**
Completion: **2005**
Category: **residential**
Location: **Seekirchen, Wallersee, Austria**
Construction materials (basic module): **steel, aluminum, linoleum**
Cost (prefabrication + installation): **155,000 Euros**
Construction time: **8 to 10 weeks to construct 7 modules**
Durability: **minimum 50 years**
Surface area: **947 sq. ft.**

Photo © Marc Haader

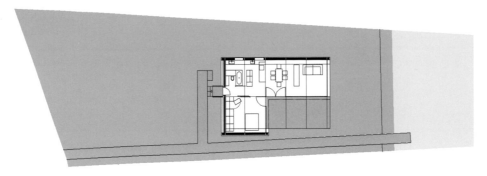

Location plan

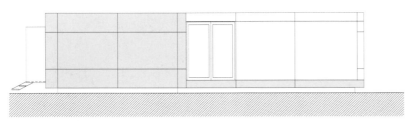

South-west elevation

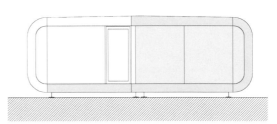

South-east elevation

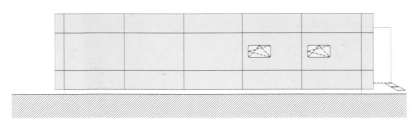
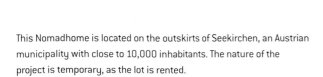

North-east elevation

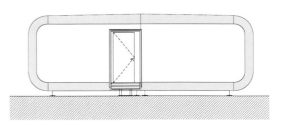

North-west elevation

This Nomadhome is located on the outskirts of Seekirchen, an Austrian
municipality with close to 10,000 inhabitants. The nature of the
project is temporary, as the lot is rented.

The team of architects stress the changeable and nomadic character of the project, given the simplicity of assembling and dismantling the modules and the ease with which they can be transported wherever they are needed.

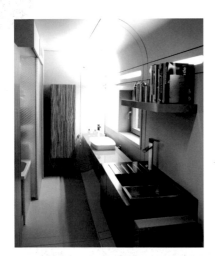

A modular home with a deck and garden can occupy approximately 947 sq. ft., of which 829 are habitable. Gerold Peham, creator of the concept, also designed the interiors.

Requirements and alternatives to complete the Nomadhome

Lot requirements:
Area measuring at least 2,153 sq. ft. — rented or owned — and connections to the sanitary network.

Basic house:
It contains a bathroom, restroom, kitchen, dining room and bedroom, with approximately 474 sq. ft. of habitable space, placed on foundations which are not too damaging to the earth.

Possibilities to extend:
The basic module can be extended by adding an unlimited number of modules to create children's areas, guest accommodation, an office or a living room.

Garage:
A porch can be added to the module to store bicycles, skis or gardening equipment.

Deck:
The basic construction can come equipped with a larch wood platform, which can also include a canopy or similar system to provide protection from the sun.

Entrance:
The entrance area, comprising a staircase and exterior hall, comes in different colors and designs.

Interiors:
The interiors can come equipped with different types of furniture, depending on the degree of quality or sophistication required.

Non-residential use:
Nomadhome also offers solutions for commercial spaces. For the 250th anniversary of the birth of Mozart in 2006, a 237 sq. ft. prototype Nomadhome was used as an information point and ticket office for the events celebrated. In the winters of 2007 and 2008, Nomadhomes were also used as commercial prototypes during *skidome* celebrations in Austria.

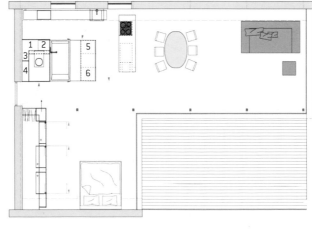

1. Technical room
2. Washing machine
3. Air-conditioning
4. Electrical system
5. Sink
6. Fridge

Plan of basic house   0   1   2

architects imagined a future with communities or towns being created by a succession of Nomadhomes, in which the inhabitants would be the true nomads of the 21st century. In addition, there is the possibility, in time, to equip the modules with solar energy systems and storage for rainwater.

REF-RING

Yasuhiro Yamashita/ Atelier Tekuto

The house is located 2 miles from Kamakura, an area in natural surroundings which is a vacation retreat close to Tokyo. The owners are a young family who like unusual architecture and they wanted a space which was unique and fun. With this in mind, the architects have created a home where the sense of space is affected by a strong feeling of ambiguity. The arrangement of panels at strange angles creates tri-dimensional areas, as if the house were twisted. The structure of the property is based on two rings twisted together, and is made of wooden panels. These axes make the space appear bigger.

This project has explored the constructive and shaping possibilities of the wooden panel developed by Yasuhiro Yamashita in collaboration with structural engineer Jyo-Ko. The panel combines various functions: structural, thermal insulation, waterproofing, and superficial finish. The laminated panels of wood, measuring 0.39 ft x 2.36 ft x 9.84 ft (up to 16.40 ft) have a hole through which a steel cable prestresses the panels. This construction method has been practiced in the factory.

REF-RING

Architect: **Yasuhiro Yamashita/Atelier Tekuto**
Completion: **2005**
Category: **residential**
Location: **Zushi, Kanagawa, Japan**
Construction materials: **wood, prestressed wooden structure**
Cost (prefabrication): **169,200 Euros**
Construction time: **15 months**
Durability: **decades**
Surface area: **691 sq. ft.**

Photo © Makoto Yoshida

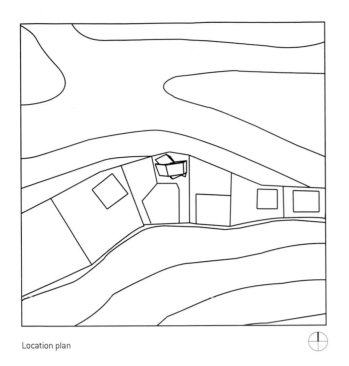

Location plan

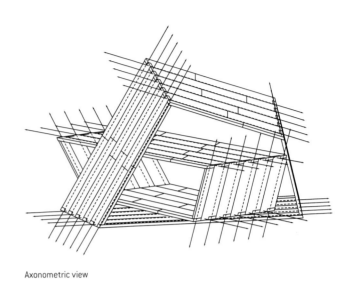

Axonometric view

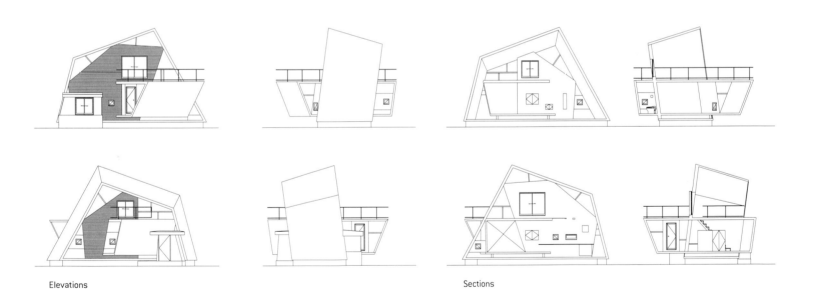

Elevations

Sections

The architect's four reference concepts have been reflection, materials, abstract quality and sensory perception. According to him, if the building is experienced on not only a visual level, but also using the senses of touch and smell, the depth and ambiguity of the property increase, boosting the inorganic abstractness of the house.

The difficult appreciation of the visual lines creates a dissonance, as human perception is usually based on horizontal and perpendicular planes.

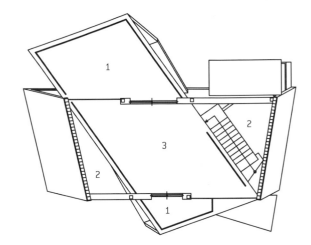

Second floor

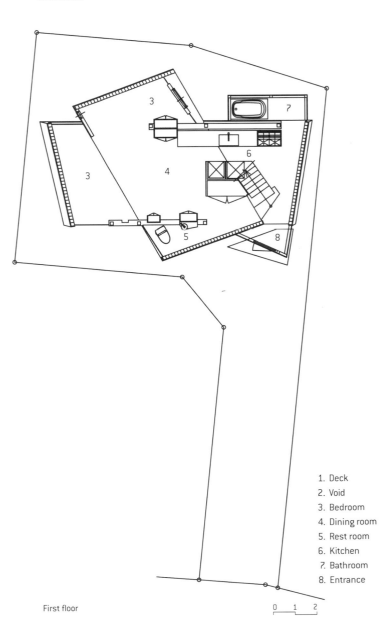

The lot measures 1,367 sq. ft. The use of wood inside provides an organic warmth in a design which is not particularly cozy, regardless of who is living in the house.

1. Deck
2. Void
3. Bedroom
4. Dining room
5. Rest room
6. Kitchen
7. Bathroom
8. Entrance

First floor

0   1   2

HEDGE BUILDING

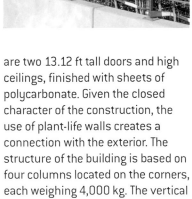

Atelier Kempe Thill
Architects & Planners

This construction was used as the Dutch pavilion at the IGA International Gardens Exhibition in Rostock in 2003, and is currently used as a cultural installation in the same city. The architect defined it as an "instant pergola", designed as if it were a "smart screen". The structure of this screen was inspired by hedges of ivy, a plant traditionally cultivated in Dutch greenhouses, planted in gardens and used in industrial environments to create vegetation walls. These hedges are usually produced in sections from 3.94 to 5.91 ft.

The building has a monolithic aspect; it comprises a rectangular floor space and the dimensions are 21.33 x 65.62 x 32.81 ft. There are two 13.12 ft tall doors and high ceilings, finished with sheets of polycarbonate. Given the closed character of the construction, the use of plant-life walls creates a connection with the exterior. The structure of the building is based on four columns located on the corners, each weighing 4,000 kg. The vertical weights are suspended by multiple columns measuring 1.97 in, which creates the visual effect that the four side walls support the building. The unpolished steel structure forms troughs which can be filled with earth, and these produce the plant-life walls which can grow up to 32.81 ft high.

HEDGE BUILDING

Architect: **Atelier Kempe Thill Architects & Planners**
Completion: **2003**
Category: **cultural installation**
Location: **Rostock, Germany**
Construction materials: **steel, Dutch ivy, polycarbonate**
Cost: **180,000 Euros (not including glass installation)**
Construction time: **2 months**
Surface area: **1,292 sq. ft.**

Photo © Ulrich Schwarz

This exhibition space is open from the spring until the end of the summer and has been used frequently to show the work of video-artists.

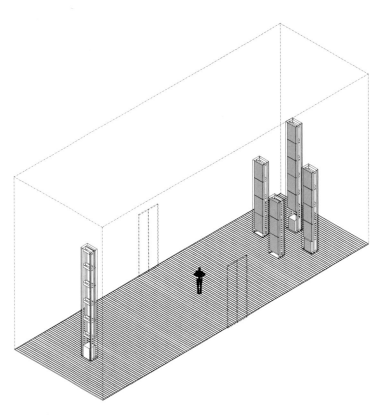

Axonometry of the video installation

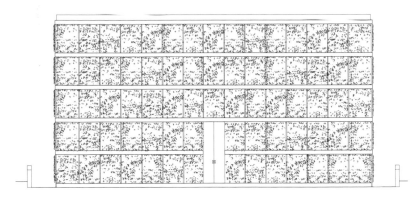

Longitudinal elevation

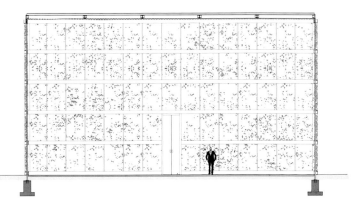

Longitudinal section

The body is formed by a geometric rectangle which is 65.62 ft long and 32.81 ft high. The principal anchorage points of the building are the four columns on the corners.

The inside is illuminated by diffused light coming in through the roof, giving the space the character of a classical museum. Dim light also filters through the sides, and the combination of the two sources of light with the movement of the leaves produces a lighting effect which increases the feeling of space.

88. Cultural installation. **Atelier Kempe Thill Architects & Planners**

The building comprises three main parts: the base, which provides the anchorage system and supports the flower beds in which the ivy grows, the plant-life surround which creates the walls, and the transparent, polycarbonate roof.

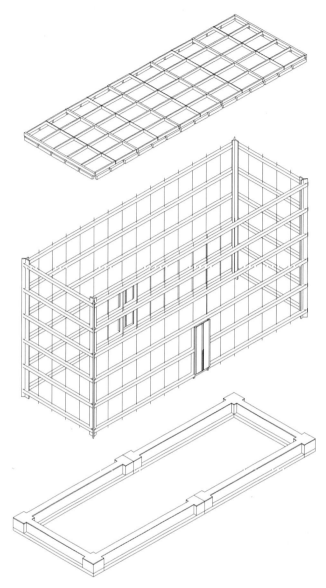

The project was designed by German architects Andre Kempe and Oliver Thill. Originally from the old GDR, they had the opportunity to represent Holland in their home country.

Fragmented view

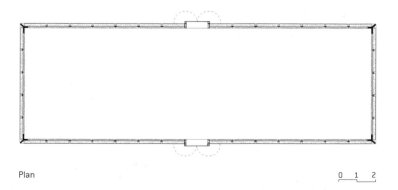

Plan

0 1 2

The smart screen is made up of a series
of identical elements, which emphasize
the industrial character of the building's
construction.

Ivy usually needs many years to grow and cover a building. The design of the area as a smart screen on which the ivy can climb enables the creation of a natural, open-air space in much less time.

U + A HOUSE

NMDA

Neil M. Denari Architects designed this prototype like a pre-designed, vertical mini hi-rise, which combines industrial design, contemporary art and *avant-garde* fashion. It was created for three different climates, using three cities as models: Los Angeles (hot and dry), Vancouver (warm and humid) and Whistler (continental and snow-covered). Despite the name of the project –

Useful (simple and economic) and Agreeable (quality prefabrication with touches of luxury) – the architect acknowledges that units could be located in remote or unusual places. The vertical mini hi-rise has a square floor-space measuring 258 sq. ft., with rounded corners. It is a compact unit which can easily be transported on a trailer, and in which all the space has been

carefully utilized. The maximum height has been fixed at 29.99 ft, which is equivalent to a home for one in North America (according to the R or R1 parameters) and Japan. The assembly of eight aluminum panels — 7.97 ft wide and 29.99 ft high — comprises the cladding of the smallest version of the house, creating maximum dimensions of 15.98 x 15.98 x 29.99 ft.

The walls and the flooring of the basic module are made up of 14 panels. The outer structure is made up of three layers: flexible plywood measuring 0.25 in, a water-proof membrane and a 16 caliber sheet of aluminum. The interior layer is 0.25 in painted plywood. The exterior finishes are patterns of paint selected by the client.

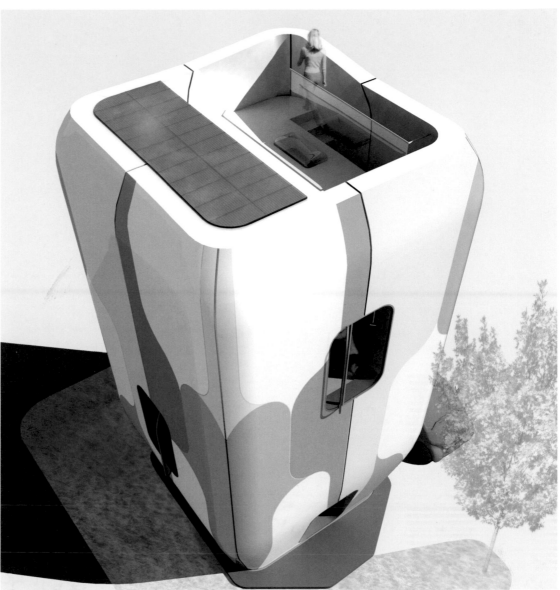

U+A HOUSE

Architect: **NMDA**
Completion: **prototype**
Category: **residential**
Construction materials: **aluminum**
Surface area: **from 657 sq. ft. to 1,789 sq. ft.**

Renderings © Neil M. Denari Architects

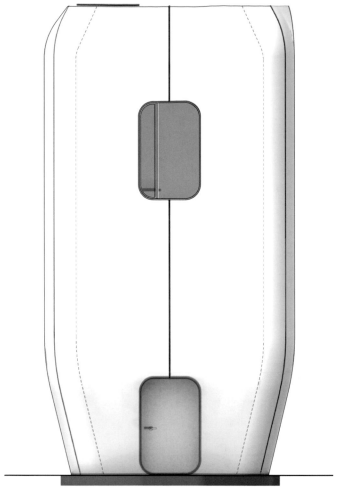

Elevation 1

Elevation 2

Assembly sequence

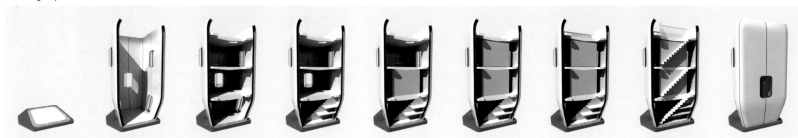

The Useful + Agreeable (U+A) in Vancouver is NMDA's answer to offering pre-fabricated houses to an emerging market of clients who value design and want a home with the same style as the other products which form part of their everyday lives.

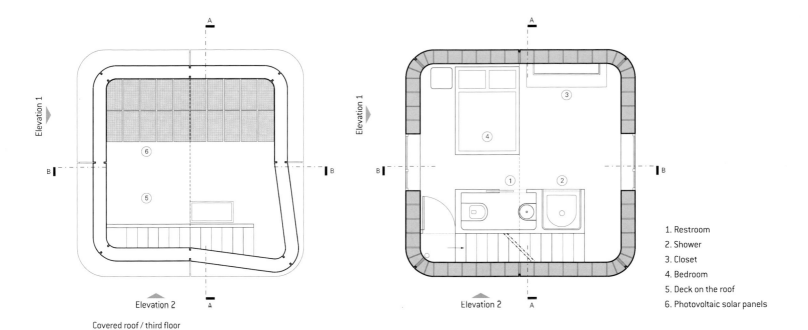

Covered roof / third floor

1. Restroom
2. Shower
3. Closet
4. Bedroom
5. Deck on the roof
6. Photovoltaic solar panels

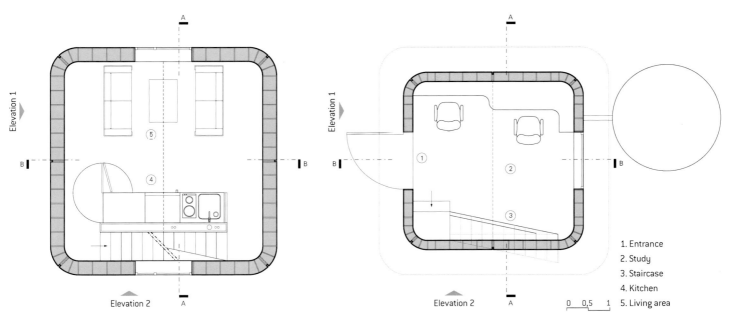

Second floor / first floor

1. Entrance
2. Study
3. Staircase
4. Kitchen
5. Living area

0   0,5   1

"The U+A pre-designed mini hi-rise is not only a tightly
designed house that uses every square inch of space
wisely, it also attempts to express this economy in its
smooth exterior surface shape, a form of industrial
design on an architectural scale." (Neil M. Denari)

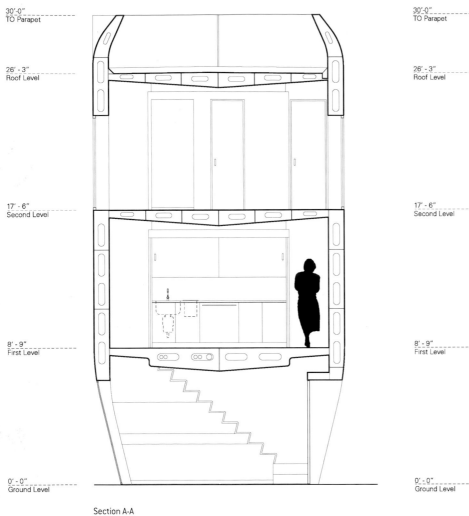

30'-0"
TO Parapet

26'-3"
Roof Level

17'-6"
Second Level

8'-9"
First Level

0'-0"
Ground Level

Section A-A

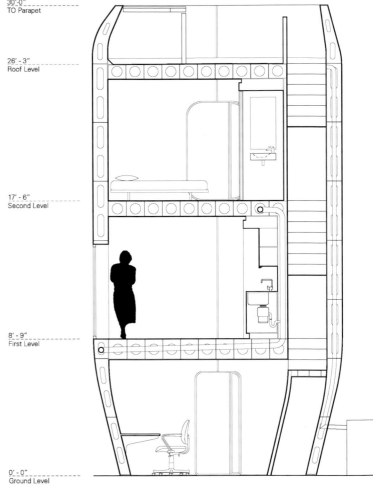

30'-0"
TO Parapet

26'-3"
Roof Level

17'-6"
Second Level

8'-9"
First Level

0'-0"
Ground Level

Section B-B

The prototype is clad in light aluminum panels with an aero-spatial design, equipped with fitted furnishings designed by NMDA. Photovoltaic panels and a system for catching rainwater can be installed on the roof terrace

The way in which the exterior cladding and the internal finishes are combined is similar to the technology used for airplane wings; a 'skin' which is rigid, compact and, at the same time, light. Unlike many prefabricated prototypes, U+A transfers the prefabrication's own style to a line of design for products on a small scale.

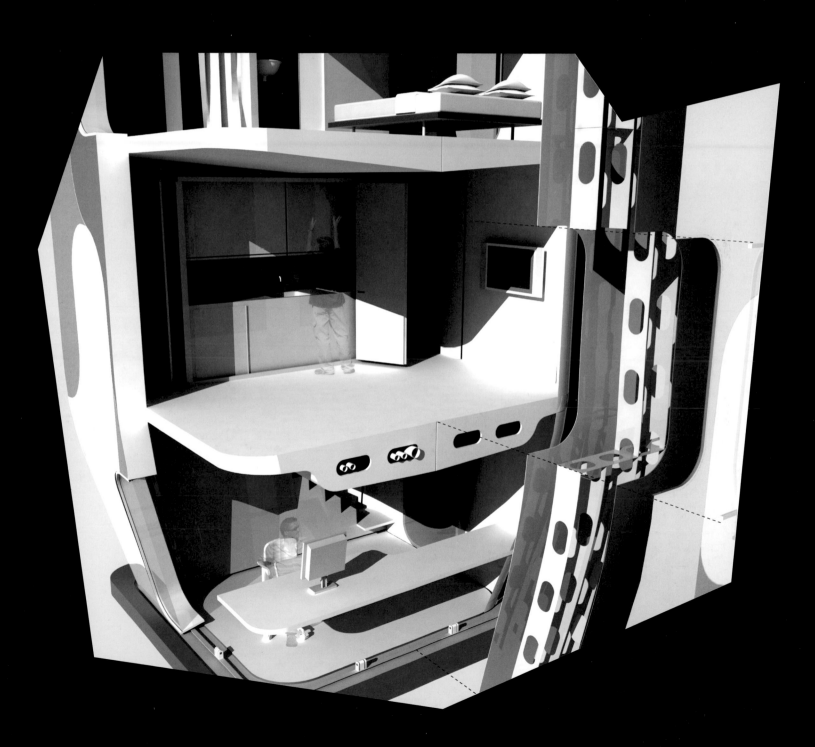

ZEROHOUSE

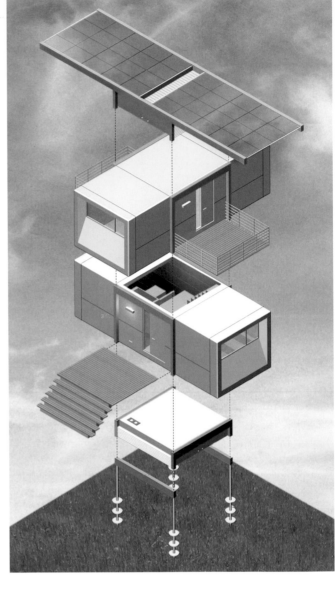

Scott Specht

Although this is only a prototype, zeroHouse is an example of sustainable housing for the present and the future. It comprises two rectangular units shaped like shipping containers, placed on top of each other on horizontal and vertical axes.

This 646 sq. ft. prototype is completely self-sufficient and does not need to be connected to either the electrical or sanitation network.

It generates its own electricity, collects and stores rainwater and treats waste material. The electrical system is generated by a network of batteries which last for a week. The temperature inside the property is regulated automatically, the sensors being controlled by a lap-top computer. In addition, zeroHouse has a highly efficient heating/air-conditioning system in both summer and winter. The daytime

and night-time areas are perfectly separated. The walls, ceiling and flooring are insulated with foam and achieve a thermal resistance rating of R-58. The windows in each of the rooms are triple-insulated and made from low energy factor glass (low-e). The external doors have vacuum sealed Aerogel panels to maintain maximum thermal resistance.

The textiles and the carpets in the property are made from natural

fibers. The illumination comes from a base of LED lights which can function for 100,000 hours of continuous use.

Rain water is stored in a 10,000 liter cistern. The system works with gravity, without the need for auxiliary pumps. Organic waste is converted to compost by a dry composter, located below the property, which needs to be emptied twice a year.

ZEROHOUSE

Architect: **Scott Specht**

Completion: **prototype**

Category: **residential**

Location: **suitable for occupation during the whole year between latitudes 36 N and 36 S. Between 47 N and 47 S partial occupation is recommended**

Construction materials: **foundation – Helical micropile anchors, stainless steel with leveling plates; structural – tubular cold-rolled steel frame sections with bonded powder-coat finish; shell – SIP panels with integrally colored dupont ECS exterior cladding**

Cost (prefabrication + transport + installation): **223,542 Euros**

Construction time: **1 day**

Surface area: **646 sq. ft. (interior), 248 sq. ft. (exterior)**

Renderings © Devin Keyes, Frank Farkash, Scott Specht

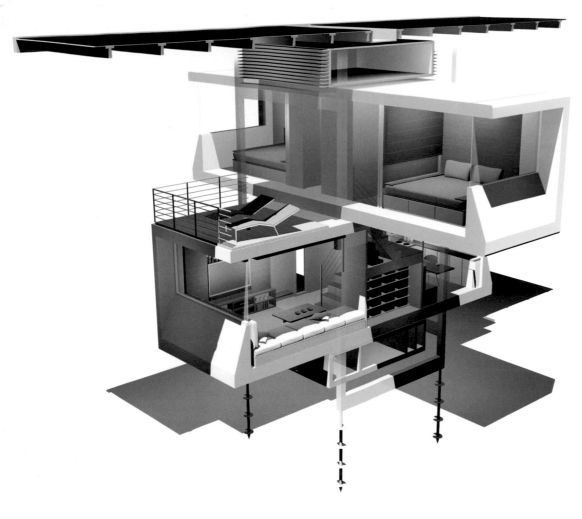

zeroHouse can be installed anywhere, as it is suspended on a four-point anchorage system which does not require excavation of earth. This makes it is suitable for protected nature areas or places where permanent foundations are prohibited. It can only be located on lots where the slope is not more than 35°, and with a phreatic stratum located at a minimum of 9.84 ft.

Bright white

Metallic silver

Deep marine

zeroHouse can be transported on two trailers and assembled in one day. The tubular structure of the house can resist winds of up to 140 m/h. The windows contain impact-resistant laminated SentryGlas. The exterior layer of the doors is reinforced with Kevlar. The finish of the cladding panels is waterproof.

Forest green

Desert red

Custom graphics

This model, designed for four adults, is equipped with a bathroom, kitchen, dining room and living area. The exterior space comprises two decks on the second floor. A flat roof creates a canopy for the terraces.

HOUSE IN REDONDO BEACH

DeMaria Design Associates

The structure of the house, located in a suburban area close to Los Angeles, is based on the shape of a 39.37 ft long ISO shipping container. The use of eight such containers has created a flexible property. It is calculated that in the United States there are a huge number of these containers lying idle in port areas. This fact, combined with the use of aerospace technology, has led to the creation of hybrid homes.

The use of containers presents a series of advantages, not only in terms of saving time and reducing the waste generated by conventional construction, but also for the structure, which is stronger than a standard framework of wood or steel. Steel containers can withstand earthquakes, common in this area, and also resist damp, fire and termites. Re-using containers also represents a reduction in the exploitation of iron reserves. The modular construction system of containers, with industrial origins, maximizes constructive efficiency. In this case, the containers arrive at the site with the mechanical, electrical and sanitary systems already incorporated. Doors like those used on airport hangers connect the interior of the house and the swimming pool. Thermal insulation is provided by ceramic material covered with a spray similar to that used by NASA for space shuttles. The roof is made of prefabricated metal panels, and the sides are clad with sheets of acrylic material. The design uses cross ventilation, which minimizes the need for air-conditioning. The energy consumed during construction is 400 kW/container.

HOUSE IN REDONDO BEACH

Architect: **DeMaria Design Associates**
Completion: **2007**
Category: **residential**
Location: **Redondo Beach, California, U.S.A.**
Construction materials: **recycled cargo shipping containers**
Cost (prefabrication + transport + installation): **308,300 Euros**
Construction time: **180 days**
Durability: **100 years (minimum)**
Surface area: **9.032 sq. ft. (lot), 3.225 sq. ft. (habitable space), 559.14 sq. ft. (garage)**

Photo © Andre Movsesyan, Christian Kienapfel

By offering designs for homes at industrial production prices, DeMaria Design Associates brings to the sphere of architecture successful concepts such as those created by Frank Lloyd Wright with his Textile Block Homes, Andy Warhol with his pictures, and McDonalds with their hamburgers.

The living area has a maximum height of 19.69 ft and opens to the exterior through folding doors similar to those used in aeronautical hangers. These doors can also serve as a canopy when they are open.

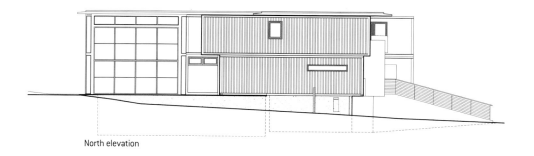

North elevation

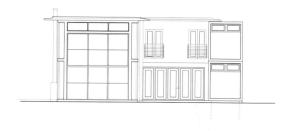

East elevation

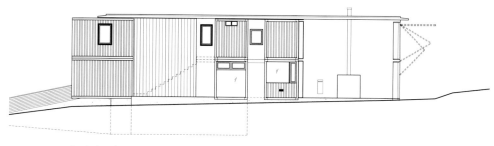

South elevation

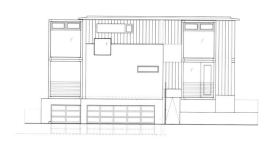

West elevation

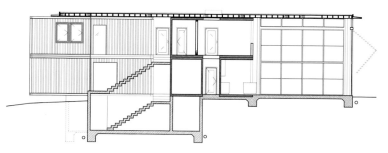

Longitudinal section

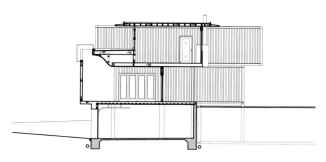

Transversal section

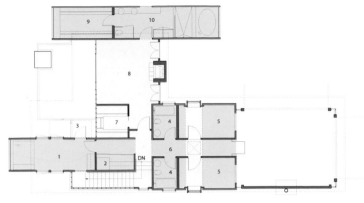

Second floor

1. Library/Guest
2. Laundry
3. Balcony
4. Bathroom
5. Bedroom
6. Hallway
7. His closet
8. Master bedroom
9. Her closet
10. Master bathroom

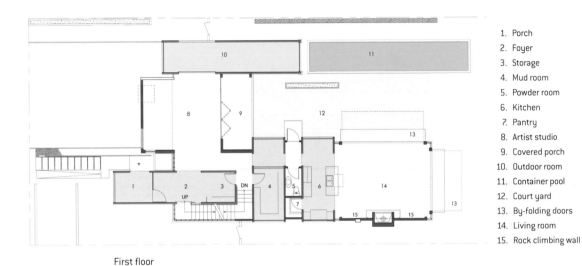

First floor

1. Porch
2. Foyer
3. Storage
4. Mud room
5. Powder room
6. Kitchen
7. Pantry
8. Artist studio
9. Covered porch
10. Outdoor room
11. Container pool
12. Court yard
13. By-folding doors
14. Living room
15. Rock climbing wall

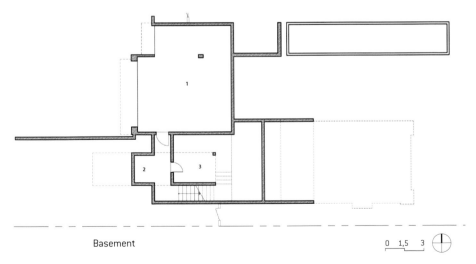

Basement

1. Garage
2. Closet
3. Hobby room

0 1,5 3

The spaces between the white painted containers, which
include the study, the master bedroom and the living
area, are defined by a wooden and steel structure. The
largest containers are divided into small compartments
which house the laundry room, the bathrooms and the
kitchen.

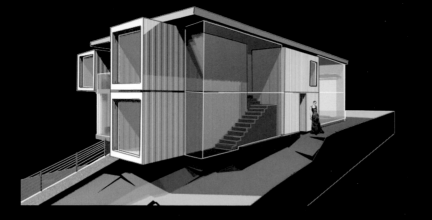

70% of the construction is carried out at the factory. DeMaria Design Associates describe the house as a "new residential product line". The architect views the construction methods used as a way to control the time and the cost of the project without affecting the quality.

The price of the house is 80.27 Euros/sq. ft., a cost which, although it could not be considered reasonable in the strictest sense, is competitive in the tailor-made housing market.

SUSTAINABLE PROTOTYPE

Studio 804

Studio 804, at the University of Kansas, is a non-profit design and construction program, aimed at recently graduated students, orientated towards prefabricated architecture. It aims to provide a solution, on a local scale, to the global problem of over-construction.

The prototype was created for the 5.4.7 Arts Center. The construction and delivery of the sustainable prototype was carried out a year after a tornado devastated the Greensburg area, which is located in one of the North-American states whose economy is based on agriculture and farming. Although the design met the specific demands of the Arts Center, the first use of the building was as a community center for the area, creating a meeting place to begin the reconstruction of the region.

Greensburg City Council ruled that all publicly-funded buildings should be reconstructed according to the US Green Building Council's LEED Platinum. Although the Arts Center was not built with public money, Studio 804 considered it logical and responsible to follow the same guidelines. The project later became the first building in the state of Kansas to be certified with the LEED Platinum.

According to the team of students who designed it, the main ecological strategies of the prototype were not damaging the lot in placing the building, the use of active and passive systems to create good bio-climatization, the use of recycled materials and, finally, the flexibility of the building's use, either as an exhibition hall, a community center, a conference room or an office.

SUSTAINABLE PROTOTYPE

Architect: **Studio 804 (University of Kansas School of Architecture and Urban Planning)**
Completion: **2008**
Category: **cultural installation**
Location: **Greensburg, Kansas, U.S.A.**
Materials: **FSC lumber, concrete, steel, glass, recycled Douglas fir and cedar**
Cost (prefabrication + transport + installation): **366,460 Euros**
Construction time: **90 days**
Durability: **50 years**
Surface area: **1,674 sq. ft.**

Photo © Studio 804

The students participated in building the prototype with the aid of specialized workers, and construction took 90 days.

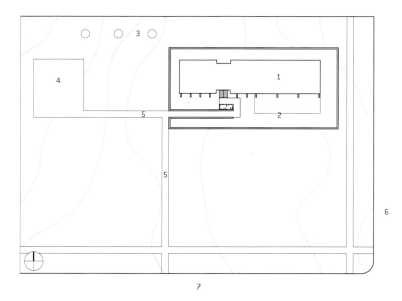

Location plan

1. Sustainable prototype
2. Elevated platform
3. Wind towers
4. Parking area
5. Path to the ramp
6. Sycamore Street
7. Wisconsin Street

The prototype is located in Greensburg, in Kiowa County in south-west Kansas. In May 2007 a tornado destroyed 95% of the city and claimed 11 lives.

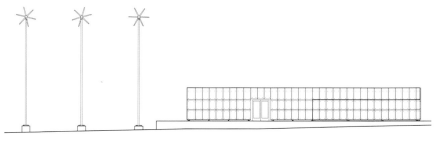

South elevation

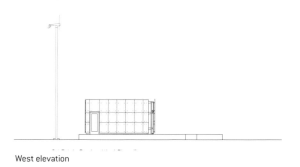

West elevation

The environmentally-friendly strategies present in the construction include:

—Passive building: south-facing, a glazed façade — which ensures a system of heat/cold transmission for thermal mass — cross ventilation, landscaped roof

—Collection of rain water

—Passive energy provides between 80 and 120% of the energy needed by the building, depending on the sunlight (according to the season) and the force of the wind

—Use of recycled cedar and Douglas fir from the military area of Sunflower

—Use of recycled cooking tops

—Use of FSC certified wood

—Surfaces free from formaldehyde and with a low VOC content

—Cellulose insulation made from a base of newspaper

—Reduced generation of waste during construction

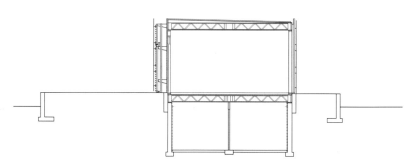

Transversal section

The floor space of the building is rectangular and comprises a main room for conferences or exhibitions, an entrance hall and a bathroom. There is also a basement.

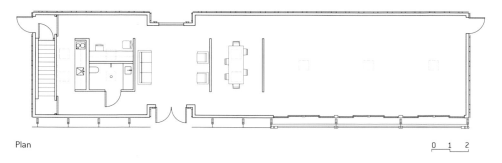

Plan

0 1 2

The external structure of the building is made from FSC certified wood, with a second skin of glass. For heating and air-conditioning, the building uses a geo-thermic pump which interchanges between an anti-freeze solution (three wells, each 200.13 ft deep) and the constant subterranean temperature. The solution is more ecologically efficient than a hot/cold pump.

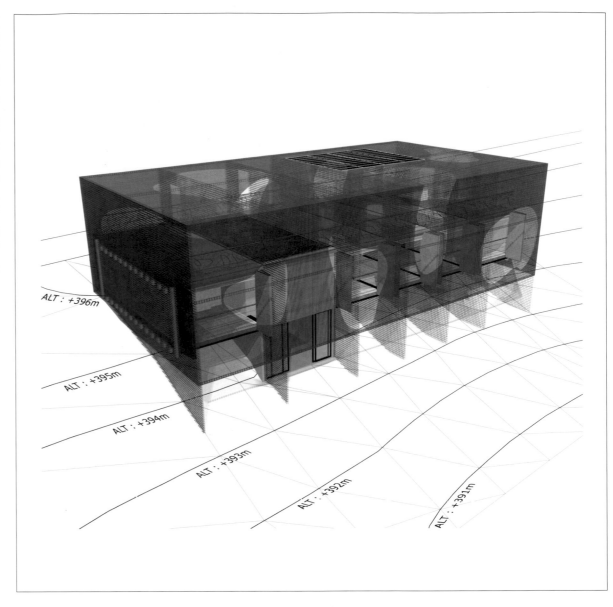

ALT : +396m
ALT : +395m
ALT : +394m
ALT : +393m
ALT : +392m
ALT : +391m

RozO Architectes

In the French colonies, the word *marronage* was used for a time to describe slaves (*maroons*) who escaped from the plantations and found their freedom in natural surroundings. This house, currently in the construction phase, uses the term to refer to the integration of future construction with its surroundings.

The location is a suburban area of La Possession, a municipal area which belongs to the department of La Réunion, an island characterized by low rainfall and well-preserved savanna. The objective of the project was to create a bio-climatic, ecological house entirely suitable to the unique characteristics of the island. Consequently, the property is compact and all the exterior spaces – including terrace, swimming pool and barbecue area – are incorporated within the structure. The body of the building has a rectangular floor area and is divided into two storeys. On the upper level there is the terrace, the swimming pool, the solarium, a green house, a laundry area and a space for barbecues. The lower level is a 'loft', adapted for tropical climates.

The structure of the building is made up of parallel sheets of concrete, spaced between 9.84 and 13.12 ft from each other, like blades. The anchorage comes from the concrete walls of the swimming pool, which do not harm the plant life of the savanna. The covering structure is made of a polyethylene mesh which generates a micro-climate inside the house and enables cross ventilation. This mesh was created using an algorithmic design that allows one to see the views through its gaps. The paving is concrete. The energy consumed during the construction was six tons of CO_2.

MARRONAZ

Architect: RozO Architectes
Completion: 2009
Category: residential
Location: La Possession, La Réunion, France
Construction materials: concrete (swimming pool and structure), metallic walls and polyethylene mesh.
Cost (prefabrication + transport + installation): 400,000 Euros
Construction time: 180 days
Durability: 15 years (polyethylene mesh), 50 years (steel structure)
Surface area: 1,615 sq. ft. (house), 1,615 sq. ft. (exterior spaces)

Renderings © RozO Architectes

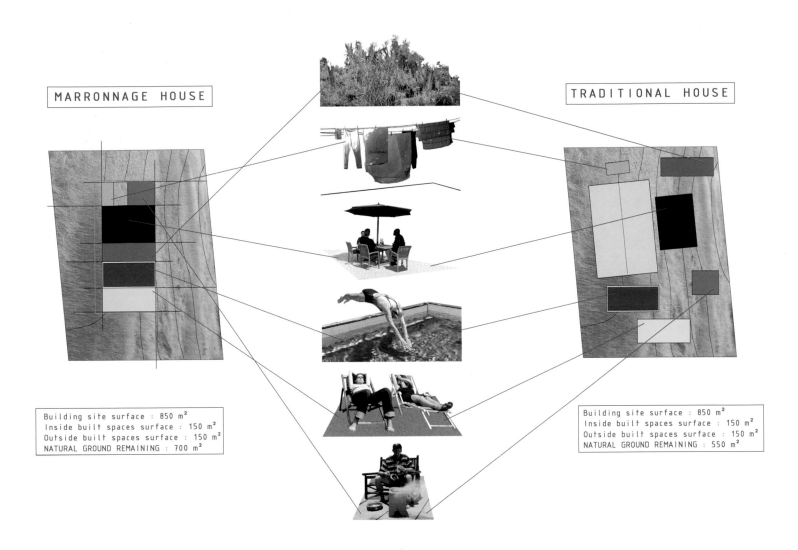

MARRONNAGE HOUSE

TRADITIONAL HOUSE

Building site surface : 850 m²
Inside built spaces surface : 150 m²
Outside built spaces surface : 150 m²
NATURAL GROUND REMAINING : 700 m²

Building site surface : 850 m²
Inside built spaces surface : 150 m²
Outside built spaces surface : 150 m²
NATURAL GROUND REMAINING : 550 m²

The covering, made from a soldered metallic mesh, enables perfect natural ventilation and allows one to see out, creating a close connection between the house and the surrounding savanna. It also protects the property against possible typhoon damage.

There is absolutely no glass in the façades. The covering around the structure comprises a green, exterior polyethylene mesh, a middle skin made from a perforated metallic frame, and finally, an internal layer with polyethylene shutters.

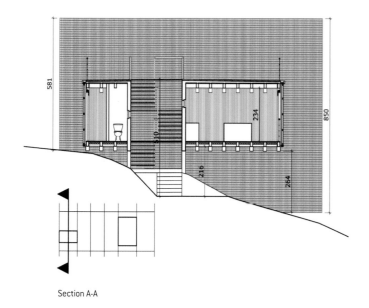

Section A-A

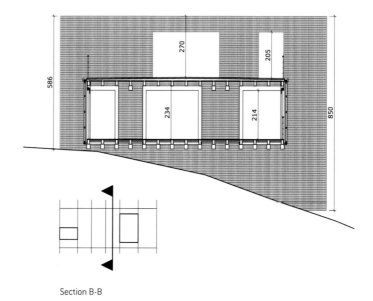

Section B-B

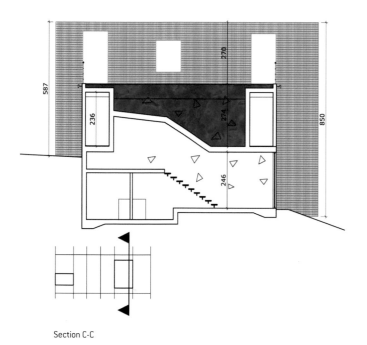

Section C-C

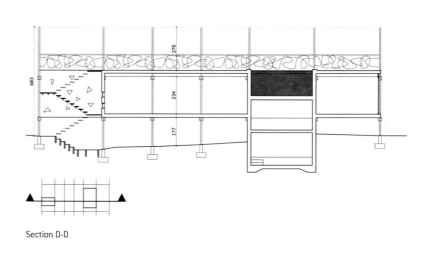

Section D-D

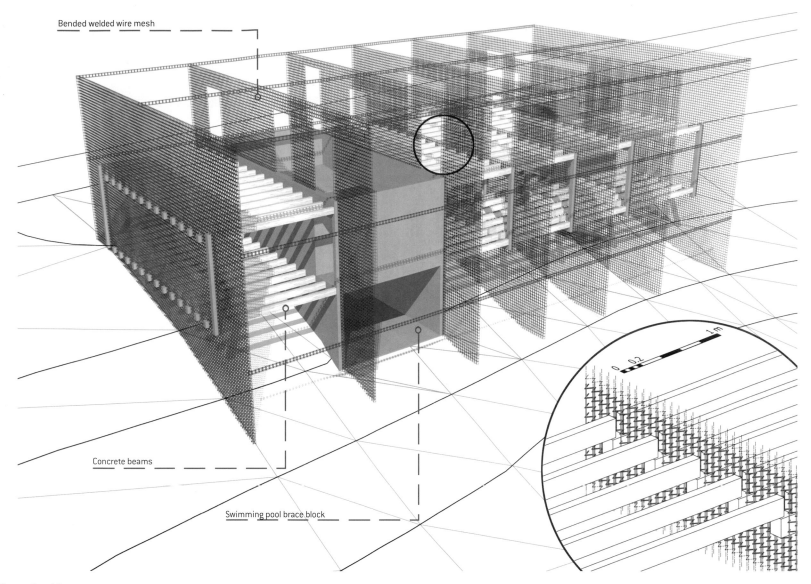

Bended welded wire mesh

Concrete beams

Swimming pool brace block

Perspective of the structure

The building uses the swimming pool brace block. This constitutes the support, from which the rest of the components of the structure are developed, such as the middle skin of perforated mesh and the concrete beams that act as braces.

The exterior plastic mesh makes the lower floor habitable, under the roof which houses the swimming pool and the main leisure-time areas.

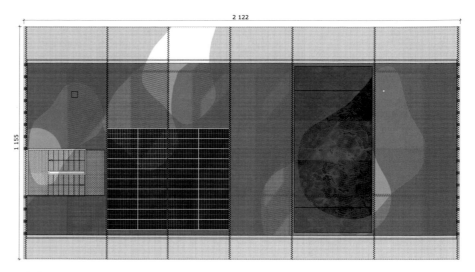

Roof

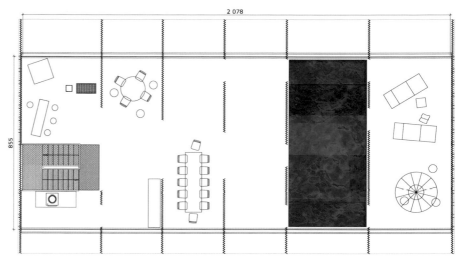

Second floor

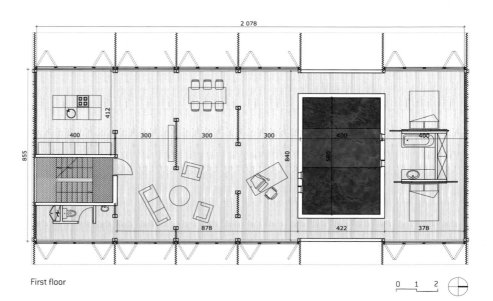

First floor

0 1 2

Renderings of the different views from inside

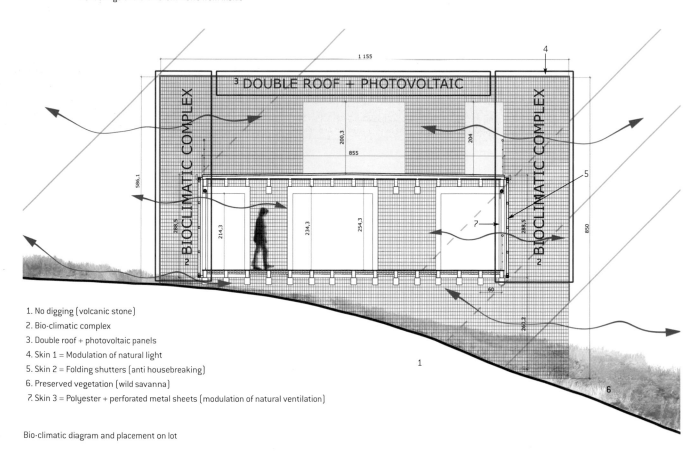

1. No digging (volcanic stone)
2. Bio-climatic complex
3. Double roof + photovoltaic panels
4. Skin 1 = Modulation of natural light
5. Skin 2 = Folding shutters (anti housebreaking)
6. Preserved vegetation (wild savanna)
7. Skin 3 = Polyester + perforated metal sheets (modulation of natural ventilation)

Bio-climatic diagram and placement on lot

BIP COMPUTER OFFICE AND SHOP

Alberto Mozó Leverington

This commercial property has been built between two houses constructed in 1936, which have been restored and are not protected by any conservation laws. The project maintained 80% of the original buildings; the two houses represent 44% of the total surface area of the lot (12,637 sq. ft.) Municipal law states that a building of up to 12 floors can be constructed on the chosen lot, which is in an urban center. The decision to erect a smaller building was a gamble by the architect, given the number of storeys permitted and considering that the owner could sell the land and a larger building could then be constructed. At the same time, this decision has repercussions in the design, creating an attractive, laminated wood structure which avoids the need to demolish existing buildings and gives the lot a renewed architectural value.
The main building is rectangular, with a roof made from a 0.02 in thick galvanized sheet. The laminated wood used for the structure comes from renewable forests, and being a totally prefabricated element, it could be dismantled and re-assembled elsewhere. If this is not the case, the beams can equally be transformed into doors and years later a door can be converted to form a table. This re-use of elements, called 'transitivity', is a valued condition in architecture.

Another advantage of the design of the structure is the choice of the same width of straight beam for the whole building. This means that the wood can be laminated quickly; enabling speed in the gluing process (in groups), efficiency in cutting the wood (catalogue) and helping with construction, as a repetitive system of framing and joining can be employed. The size of this section (3.54 x 13.46 in) was catalogued by the forest company Arauco.

BIP COMPUTER OFFICE AND SHOP

Architect: **Alberto Mozó Leverington**
Completion: **2007**
Category: **shop and office**
Location: **Santiago de Chile, Chile**
Construction materials: **pine wood**
Cost (prefabrication): **635 Euros/m²**
Construction time: **120 days**
Durability: **30 years**
Surface area: **6,802 sq. ft.**

Photo © Cristobal Palma

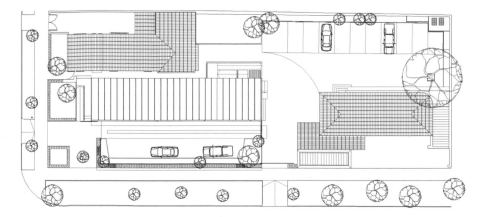

Location plan

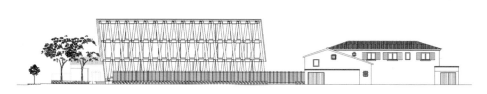

East elevation

North elevation

West elevation

South elevation

This prefabricated construction is erected on a lot housing two old buildings which have been restored. The wooden structure gives the façade a malleable character, lending the building a feeling of non-permanence.

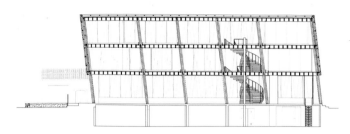

Longitudinal section

Transversal section

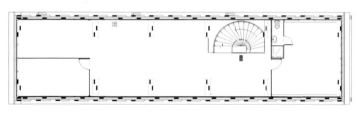

Third floor

Second floor

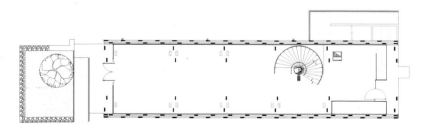

First floor

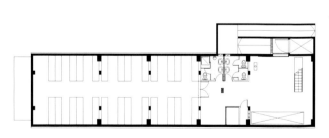

Basement

Inside, the floors are glued-down, off-white MDF, and there is a glazed façade which affords views of the exterior and lets light into the interior spaces.

Holzbox

This campus, located in rural surroundings close to the Salza River, was financed by the European Union's Leader Plus project, and economic assistance from the government of the province of Styria. The aim of the above-mentioned scheme is to encourage regional and traditional architectural development.

In 2003 Holzbox won the competition to create a modular structure, multifunctional campus. Following this, in 2004 they built the Passail campus. Wildalpen, smaller than its predecessor, is in fact an annex to the existing Wild Water Center. The building is anchored to the ground by columns. The first floor houses only the mechanical room and a storage area for maintenance materials. The main entrance is located on the second floor and is accessible by a staircase. Once inside there is a hall, which is one of the few communal areas in the building. The structure is made up of five modules with apartments, and a module of the same size which houses the communal area.

The modules have a surface of 376 sq. ft. On the sides facing east and west there are small bedrooms which can be separated from the rest of the space by sliding doors. Each module-apartment has a central area with the bathroom and kitchen. The structure of the space is open and includes built-in furniture such as bunk-beds. This produces a feeling of space although the area is small. The energy needed to acclimatize the building is 49 kWh/m^2.

WILDALPEN MOUNTAIN CAMPUS

Architect: **Holzbox**
Completion: **2006**
Category: **residential installation**
Location: **Wildalpen, Austria**
Construction materials: **wood, glass, medium density board (MDF), high density board (HPL)**
Cost: (prefabrication + transport + installation): **500,000 Euros**
Construction time: **60 days**
Durability: **decades**
Surface area: **3,466 sq. ft. (usable surface: 2,637 sq. ft.)**

Photo © Birgit Koell

The building comprises a rectangular structure anchored by concrete pillars and by the base of the staircase, with a maintenance room and other installations below.

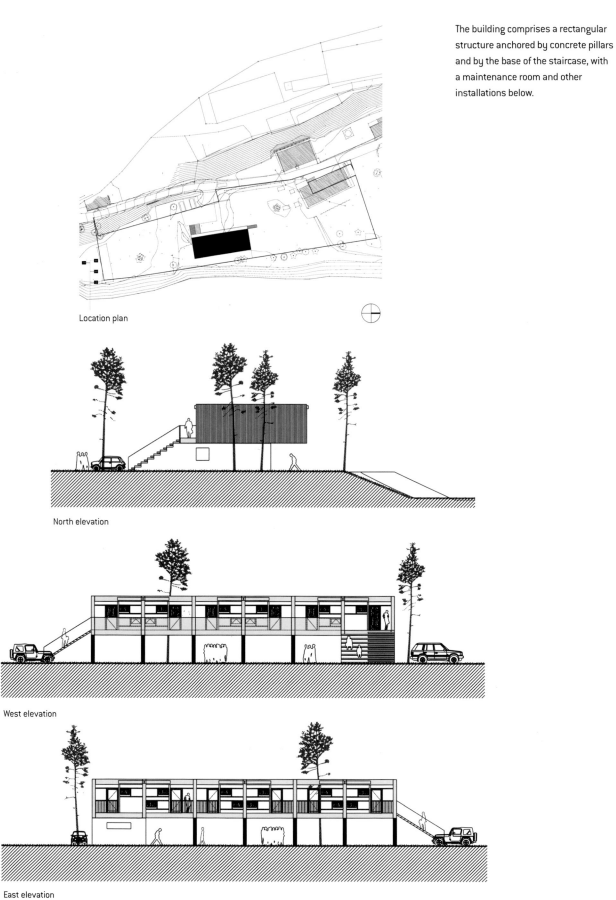

Location plan

North elevation

West elevation

East elevation

The organization of the interior spaces means that all the bedrooms receive natural light. The loggias of the module-apartments are located on the east façade.

The interiors are characterized by their functional furnishings,
which can be adapted to continually changing residents.
The campus is used mainly by visitors to the Wild Water
Center, located in Wildalpen, 1,991.47 ft above sea level. The center
attracts those keen on climbing, hiking, kayaking and rafting.

The module-apartment is made up of a central space housing the bathroom, an integral kitchen, two bedrooms at opposite angles — each room measuring 64 sq. ft. — and a 204 sq. ft. living area, completed with a loggia of almost 22 sq. ft.

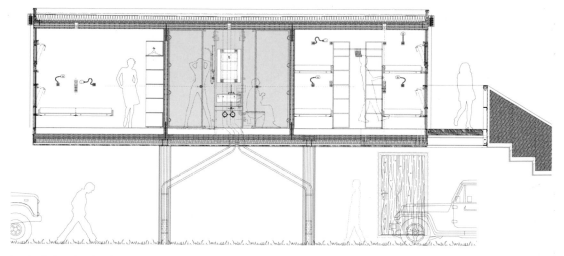

Longitudinal section of module-apartment

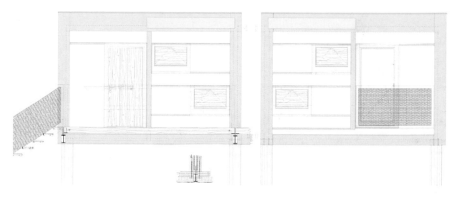

Transversal sections of module-apartment

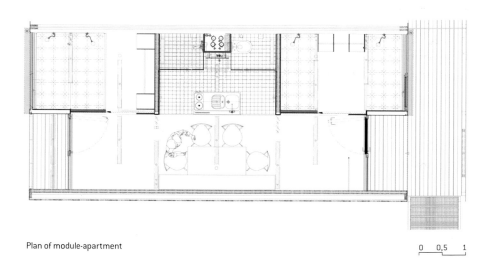

Plan of module-apartment

0   0,5   1

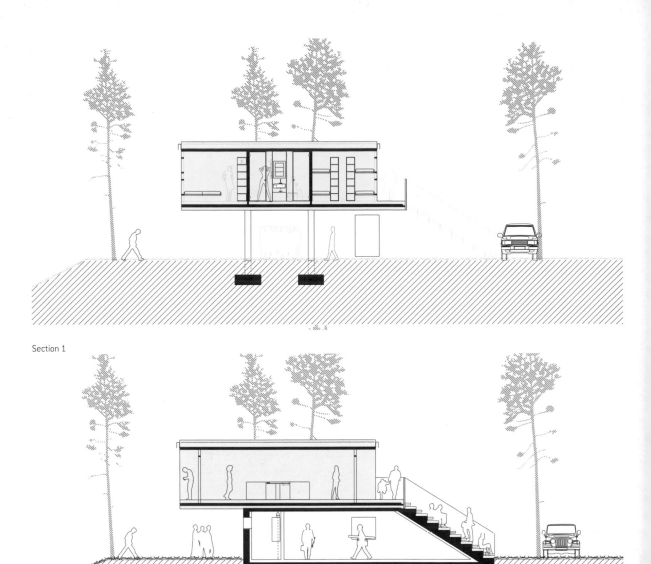

Section 1

Section 2

The first floor, open to a main 'floating' space, is the meeting point in the event of rain. The columns which anchor the building are made of concrete.

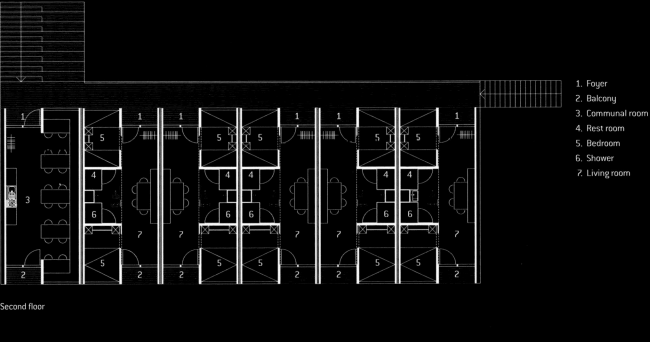

1. Foyer
2. Balcony
3. Communal room
4. Rest room
5. Bedroom
6. Shower
7. Living room

Second floor

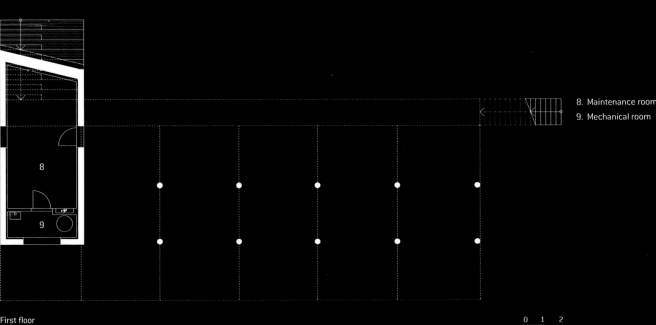

8. Maintenance room
9. Mechanical room

First floor

0 1 2

Caramel Architekten,
F. Stiper Designer

Voestalpine, a company which used to be state-owned, needed a certain time to improve its image of low productivity, inflexibility and non-ecological practices. The business was re-structured and absorbed by an Austrian group with an international market. Voestalpine has always specialized in the production of high-quality steel, and it currently also processes and manufactures products with steel finishes. In terms of control processes, protection of the environment has become one of the company's priorities. Caramel Architekten won the competition organized by Voestalpine to create platforms for those visiting the company's main sites. These visitors could be anything from a group of school children to a small party of businessmen. The architects have developed a standard module as a basic element for each platform. The modules have a symmetrical shape and can be combined randomly or according to the size and shape needed by the client.

The modules have been painted a blue similar to that of the company logo; they have all been constructed in the factory and assembled on site. The interior of each module has different levels to enable optimum visibility from all angles. The compartment has retro-illuminated panels. During the visits, and following the presentation of a documentary on the monitors installed there, the glass panels become transparent and the visitor can follow the evolution of the processes in the factory.

VISIT PLATFORM VOESTALPINE

Architect: **Caramel Architekten, F. Stiper Designer**
Completion: **2006**
Category: **promotional installation**
Location: **Linz, Austria**
Construction materials: **steel, glass**
Cost (prefabrication + transport + installation): **600,000 Euros**
Construction time: **3 months**
Durability: **50 years**
Surface area: **478 sq. ft.**

Photo © Caramel Architekten

Position of the blast furnaces

3D view of the roof and the suspension points

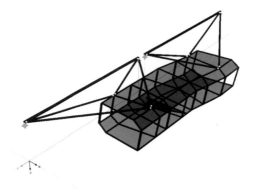

Structure in 3D

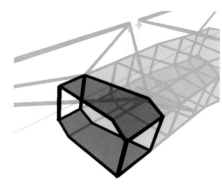

Standard module in 3D

The platform is made up of different welded modules which have previously been cut and designed in the factory. Caramel Architekten designed a structure to be hung, protected from the installations, which could adopt a hybrid form as the client required.

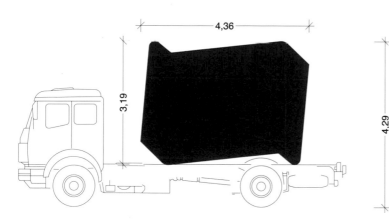

Illustration of transport of module using truck

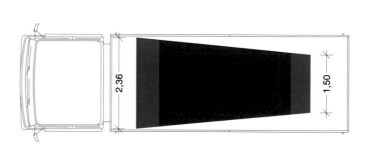

The prefabricated modules can be transported by truck and assembled on site. Their shape and final placement depend on the requirements of the client and of the Voestalpine building in which they are to be installed.

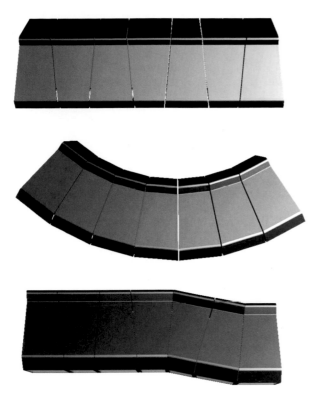

Concept of modular structure

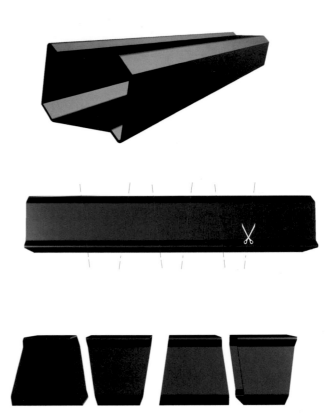

Diagram of production of modules

Standard module with furnishings in perspective

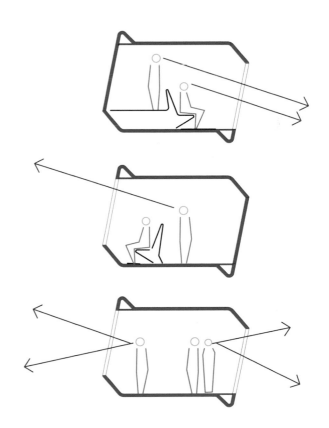

Section of possible views from the platform

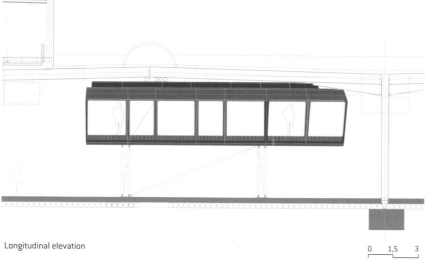

Longitudinal elevation

0   1,5   3

140. Promotional installation. Caramel Architekten, F. Stiper Designer

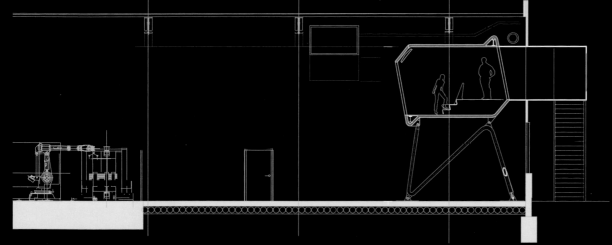

Transversal section

141 Promotional installation. VISIT PLATFORM VOESTALPINE

AUGARTEN CINEMA

Main projection room
Projection room
Technical room
Exhibition room
Exhibition room
Control room
Office
Restaurant
Foyer

Spatial diagram

Alternative proposals

Oskar Leo Kaufmann & Albert Rüf

This project was part of a competition carried out for the Filmarchiv Austria institution, contracted to collect movies and cinematographic documents with cultural importance for Austrian audio-visual history. The objective was to create a cinema and movie library with a modular structure using a frame made only of scaffolding. The winner of the competition was the Delugan Meissl studio.

The featured project was a temporary construction, as it is only during the summer months that the Augarten Park offers open-air cinema sessions, known as 'cinema under the stars'. The park, comprising 52 hectares, is a tourist attraction as it houses the Augarten Palace and a porcelain factory.

Like any prefabricated structure, the framework proposed by Oskar Leo Kaufmann and Albert Rüf can easily be dismantled and stored away until needed the following year. The architectural team designed a construction which would house two projection rooms of different sizes, a foyer, a restaurant, an office, a technical projection room and two exhibition rooms.

The rectangular-shaped structure can be up to seven storeys high, with a deck on the roof measuring more than 2,152 sq. ft. The rest of the rooms can be integrated in the central part, with staircases at the sides.

AUGARTEN CINEMA

Architect: **Oskar Leo Kaufmann & Albert Rüf**
Completion: **competition (2006)**
Category: **cultural installation**
Location: **Vienna, Austria**
Construction materials: **steel (scaffolding)**
Surface area: **approximately 10,760 sq. ft.**

Renderings © Oskar Leo Kaufmann & Albert Rüf

Bird's-eye view

Model of location plan

1. Foyer
2. Ticket office
3. Café
4. Main projection room
5. Access to the office
6. Office
7. Projection room
8. Exhibition room
9. Rest room

Longitudinal section

Transversal section

FILM
ARCHIV
AUSTRIA

Using constructions from the world of entertainment as a model, the studio designed a type of 'cinema tower' — a cultural installation arranged vertically.

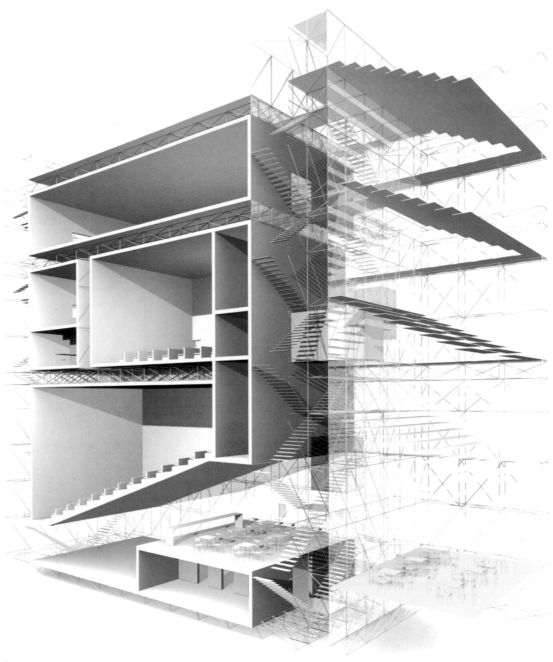

Perspective

The central part of the building houses the projection and
exhibition rooms, the meeting area and the office. There are
staircases on either side which give access to the other floors.

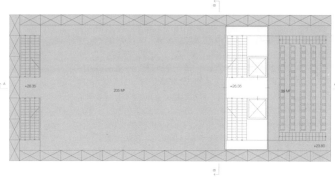

Seventh floor

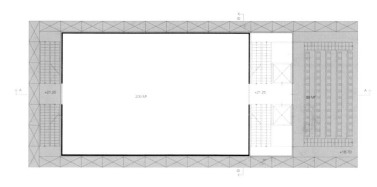

Sixth floor

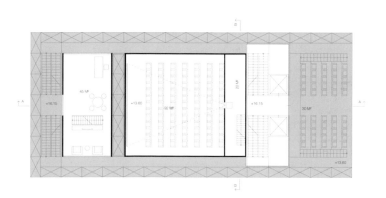

Fifth floor (second level)

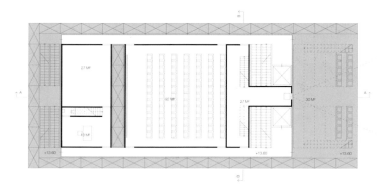

Fifth floor

0 3 6

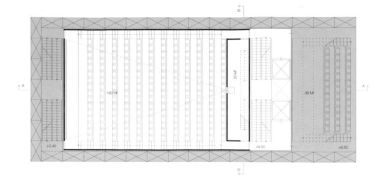

Fourth floor

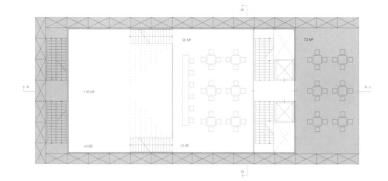

Second floor

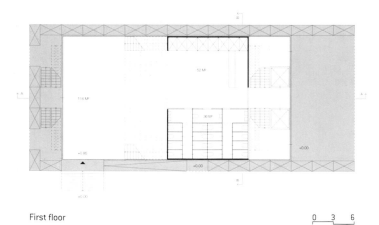

First floor

0 3 6

The main projection room is on the fourth floor. One storey
above there is a small projection room for art films.

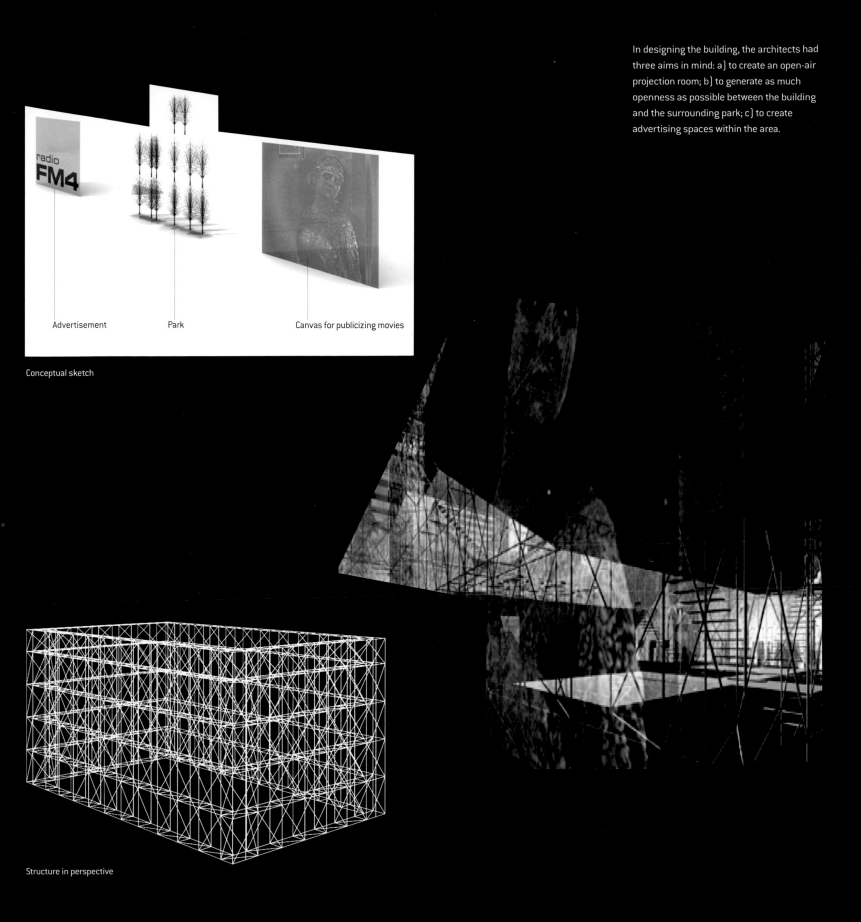

In designing the building, the architects had three aims in mind: a) to create an open-air projection room; b) to generate as much openness as possible between the building and the surrounding park; c) to create advertising spaces within the area.

radio FM4

Advertisement   Park   Canvas for publicizing movies

Conceptual sketch

Structure in perspective

FAWOOD CHILDREN'S CENTER

SMC Alsop

Located in the neighborhood of Harlesden in North London, the Fawood Children's Center is a pleasant, healthy space for pre-school children. The Stonebridge Housing Action Trust (HAT) wanted to extend an existing nursery and social center called the Evan Davis Nursery. The new nursery, for infants aged 3 to 5, autistic children and minors with special needs, also includes classrooms for adults. This 'briefing' follows the guidelines proposed by the authorities, which wanted the space to combine play areas and teaching spaces, and to provide facilities for the local community, the parents and the children's carers.

SMC Alsop's proposal differs greatly from the usual design for this type of center. Traditional nurseries tend to have spaces for children in first floor accommodation, surrounded by open-air play areas, although the British climate means these often cannot be used for most of the year. SMC Alsop's design enables total integration of the interior and exterior spaces. The main structure of the complex is formed by 20 shipping containers provided by Container City (www.containercity.com), which patented modular systems for the creation of reasonably-priced, flexible housing.

The premises include a trapezoidal square. The roof is partially translucent and has horizontal bands running from one side to the other. The walls are made of stainless steel metallic mesh, the density of the mesh varying according to the height. The interior rooms which are not used for playing are air-conditioned.

FAWOOD CHILDREN'S CENTER

Architect: **SMC Alsop**
Completion: **2004**
Category: **educational establishment**
Location: **London, United Kingdom**
Construction materials: **20 shipping containers, metallic mesh, polycarbonate**
Cost (prefabrication): **682,000 Euros**
Construction time: **20 weeks (prefabrication) + 7 days (installation)**
Durability: **30 years**
Surface area: **13,132 sq. ft.**

Photo © Alan Lai

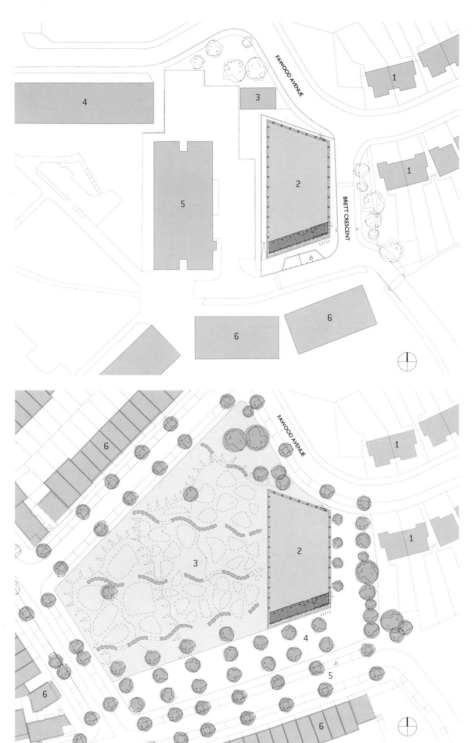

The proposed master plan involves demolishing existing residential areas and building a park in the area adjoining the educational complex.

Flexibility is among the advantages of the construction technique used, achieved through the possibility of combining 20 containers. It also provides a solution to the reduced construction time and low budget for the project.

154. Educational establishment. **SMC Alsop**

Among the spaces for children inside the building are
a picnic area, a tunnel made from willow branches, a stage,
a tree-house and a garden with a small pond.

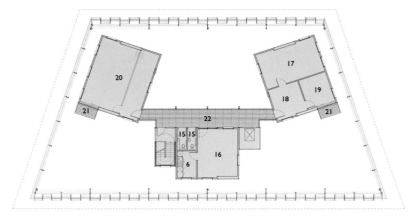

Third floor

1. Entrance terrace
2. Reception
3. Administration office
4. Faculty office
5. Meeting room
6. Kitchen
7. Bathroom and changing room for children
8. Bathroom for the disabled
9. Children's nursery
10. Shop
11. Garbage cans
12. *Yurt*
13. Toy library
14. Children's bathroom/laundry
15. Adults' bathroom
16. Staff room
17. Nursery administration office
18. Nursery reception
19. Nursery co-ordination office
20. Computer room
21. Balcony
22. Walkway

A. Square
B. Willow-branch tunnel
C. Enclosure
D. Magnolia
E. Birch
F. Climbing wall
G. Planted troughs with climbers
H. Stage
I. Soft-surface play area
J. Games room
K. Bicycle circuit
L. Sand-pit
M. Garden
N. Warehouse

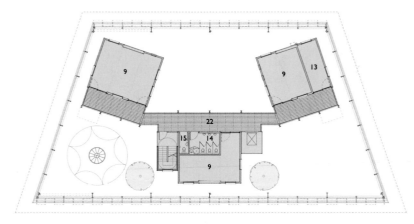

Second floor

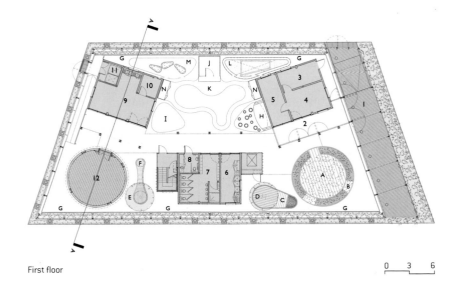

First floor

0   3   6

While the lower part of the wall uses a denser mesh to enhance the building's security, the upper levels feature curtains of lightweight mesh that are modulated into rippling curves by elliptical colored acrylic 'lozenges'. To the obvious delight of the children, light will filter through the mesh, casting colored shadows onto the internal floor and wall surfaces. Vertical creeping clematis and vines are planted on the inside of the mesh screen at the lower level on the east and west elevations to modulate further the internal and external environments. On the outside, planting and hard landscaping with up-lighting will form a buffer zone with the future park. The roof of the structure is formed of a mix of opal polycarbonate roof cladding and bright pink powder-coated profiled steel cladding on galvanized steel purlins and portal frame. Among the different attractions for the children is a *yurt*, inspired by those found in Mongolia. All the existing equipment, including sensorial and interactive installations, was designed by SMC Alsop with the collaboration of artist Joanna Turner.

The use of shipping containers reinforces the prefabricated theme of the whole project, as represented by the prefabricated structure of the roof and the metallic mesh walls. These, located in the east and west façades, are decorated with brightly colored, curved pieces in relief.

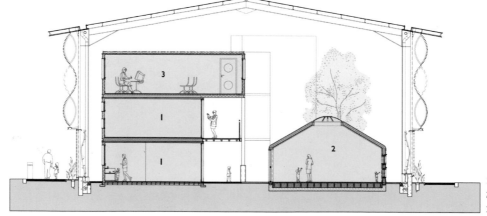

1. Children's nursery
2. *Yurt*
3. Computer room

Section A-A

The containers are stacked to create three storeys, connected by walkways, balconies, an elevator and stairs, and they comply with the safety requirements and thermal comfort necessary for a children's center.

POSTFOSSIL NURSERY

Despang Architekten

This educational center is located in Hanover, in a suburb created in the 1950s. The new nursery replaced one which was located on the same site for more than 30 years. The client for the project was the department of municipal and social installations for the city of Hanover. The plan was for a nursery to accommodate a maximum of

75 children, designed according to the guidelines set out by the German *passivhaus* certification. The building is rectangular and the south façade is a curved glass wall-curtain which makes maximum use of the sunlight, with the trees in the area providing a natural screen for the building. The structural system is a light frame prefabricated wood platform

system, with thermally disconnected TJI trusses as the peripherical members. On the north façade, the 15.75 in shell is made of sheets of plywood, with triple-glazed interior windows incorporated. The use of these sheets enables transparency between the interior and exterior, despite the fact that the north

façade has a clearly closed character, while the south façade is open. Inside the walls are made of a birch plywood covering, the ceiling is acoustically insulated with wood shavings and the floors are brown linoleum. The structure of the roof is made of wooden beams.

"POSTFOSSIL" NURSERY

Architect: **Despang Architekten**
Completion: **2007**
Category: **educational installation**
Location: **Hanover, Germany**
Construction materials: **wooden frame, glass, TJI (Truss joist I-beam) with cellulose insulation**
Cost (prefabrication + transport + installation): **925,000 Euros**
Construction time: **30 days (prefabrication), 7 days (installation)**
Durability: **decades**
Surface area: **6,964 sq. ft. (total area), 4,123 sq. ft. (usable surface)**

Photo © Olaf Baumann

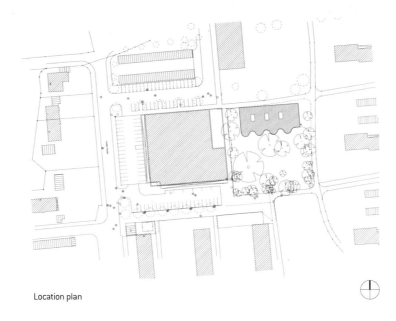

Location plan

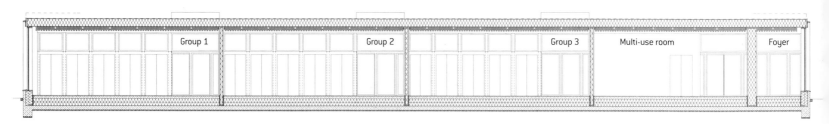

Group 1   Group 2   Group 3   Multi-use room   Foyer

Longitudinal section

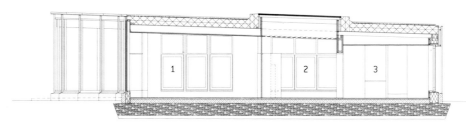

1. Class for small children
2. Corridor
3. Rest room

Transversal section

The nursery is located in an area where dense urbanization is mixed with green areas. In the 1970s there was a nursery on this lot. It was only intended to be temporary, and deteriorated over time.

162. Educational installation. Despang Architekten

The prefabricated main structure is made of wood with cellulose insulation. The interior arrangement follows bio-climatic principles, so that the area facing north is more closed, while the south facing areas make the most of the sunlight.

North elevation

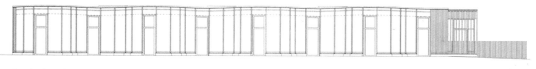

South elevation

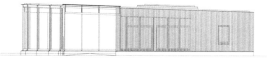

East elevation

West elevation

Martin Despang:

"The public always seems to be in favor of what we call the 'TOYS 'R' US' mentality, which means that the bigger, the brighter and the more colorful the better. The planning team still believes in the old 'play in the muddy outdoors' approach, where the complex simplicity of the textures and patterns of nature are much more inspiring than capitalistic driven human imagination could ever be. This has been an ongoing discussion in all educational projects in the past, and so it was here, when it came to presentations in panels and committees. Luckily the client was very open and willing to follow us into the mud!"

"The children and the teachers have just moved in. After having witnessed every step of the building process, they expressed their excitement about the healing quality of this healthy space." Asked about his favourite aspect or quality of the building: "The fact that the Postfossil building is naturally adapting the first postfossil generation for a future in challenging both eco — and architectural — friendliness."

The service areas are located on the north side and connected to the living areas and the bedrooms by a corridor which is large enough for the children to play in. The interior of the center receives plenty of natural light.

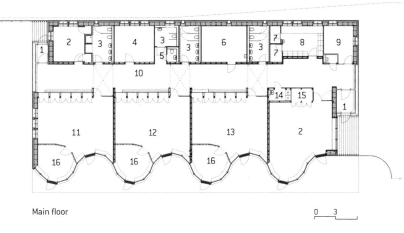

Main floor

0   3

1- Foyer
2- Multi-use room
3- Rest room
4- Staff room
5- Rest room for the disabled
6- Mechanical room
7- Pantry
8- Kitchen
9- Office
10- Corridor
11- Group 3
12- Group 2
13- Group 1
14- Laundry
15- Closet
16- Room for small groups

The use of sheets of wood on the west and north façades creates patterns of light and shadow which capture the children's imagination.
The nursery is open from 8 am to 4 pm.

Andrew Maynard Architects

Andrew Maynard Architects designed a computerized library as a cultural center for the community — an automated space which changes the concept of giving and taking actual books. The idea comes from facts proven in developed countries: books are no longer so readily available, and there is a growing separation between book and reader. Access to books on shelves is becoming more virtual. This gradual change, particularly obvious in countries like Japan, has taken place to avoid theft, physical damage to books and disorganization of the catalogue. With this library, the architectural design reinforces the exchange of information. Although the search for books and their delivery is mechanized, the design of the system turns the request for a book into a virtual experience: the hard-drive of a computer is a catalyst for a large collection of books.

The book as an object acts here as a metaphor for the whole project. It is not only a case of its location on the shelf. The use of glazed façades turns the book-shelves into a visual reference: they can be seen from different public areas, so the passers-by adopted the library as the city's cultural symbol, and in addition, it serves to orientate them. This proposal clearly supports the digitalization of information, a point of interest as much for now as for the future. The design creates a bridge between the digital and reality, as the mechanical action turns into a robotic act of searching for and delivering information.

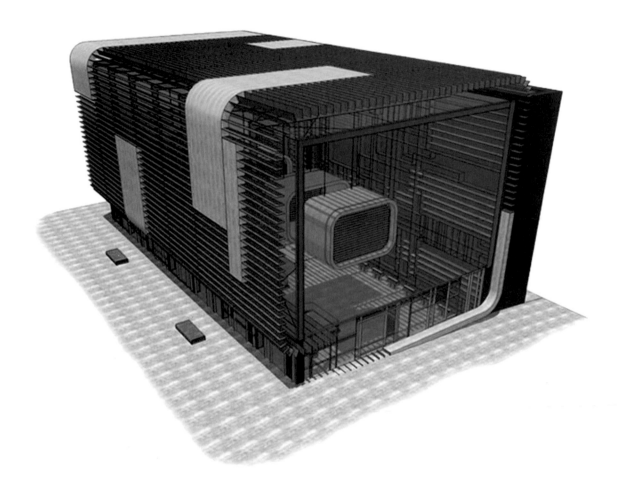

LIBRARY IN JAPAN

Architect: **Andrew Maynard Architects**
Completion: **competition**
Category: **cultural installation**
Location: **rural area in Japan**
Construction materials: **wood**

Renderings © Andrew Maynard Architects

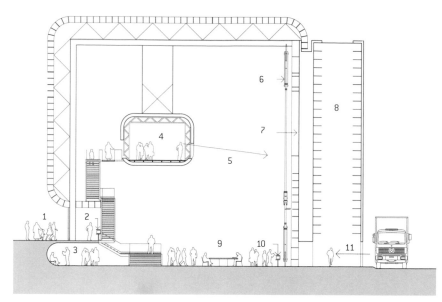

1. Entrance
2. Quick-order terminal
3. Reading and children's room
4. Seating areas
5. Customers can see the book-shelves at all times
6. Robotic arm
7. Book-shelves
8. Area for staff and book archive
9. Room for reading and studying
10. Terminal for orders
11. Point for collecting books

Transversal section

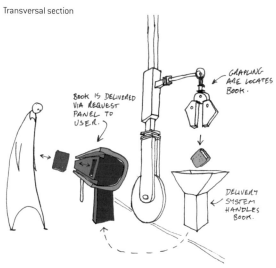

Conceptual diagram of book delivery point

Delivery of books in study room

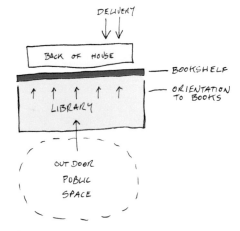

Schematic plan

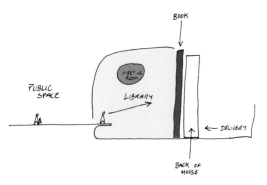

Schematic section

Unlike many prefabricated prototypes, a pre-designed one transfers the style of the prefabricated structure to a plan which is more typical of a small-scale product style.

The channeling of information in a computerized way is the real impulse of the design. The structure of the building (made from slats and sheets of wood), the modules (seating areas), the shelves and the furnishings are all prefabricated.

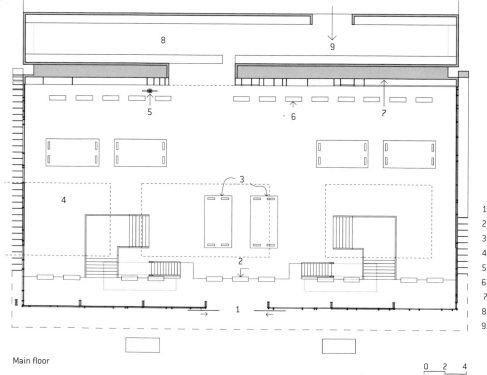

Main floor

0   2   4

1. Entrance
2. Quick-order terminal
3. Book delivery point in study room
4. Seating area (upper floor)
5. Robotic arm
6. Terminal for orders
7. Book-shelves
8. Area for staff and book archive
9. Point for collecting books

Each time a book is chosen, a robot finds it and delivers it to the customer. Just like the hard-drive of a computer, the jointed arm registers and updates information continuously.

Computerized storage
as catalyst for
retrieving information

ECO-VILLE

OMD

This ecological residential complex, still in the design phase, offers a flexible combination of homes and work spaces, originally planned to house artists. The initial design, created for downtown Los Angeles, comprised 40 OMD Portable Houses which could be placed or stacked in landscaped lots. OMD have also started to renovate some old warehouses in the area to create new buildings in which people can live and work.

The complex consists of rectangular homes, based on the shape of shipping containers, with the possibility of stacking them on top of each other. The arrangement of the interior spaces would be a workshop on the first floor, with a living area and bedroom on the second floor, and access to a roof garden.

Among the sustainable measures used are landscaping, comprising plants which are not affected by heat, communal gardens, energy efficient tank-less water heaters, radiant heat ceiling panels on the roof, and translucent polycarbonate sheets, balanced with high-end amenities like the iPort integrated sound system, Boffi kitchens, and Duravit bathroom fixtures. The floors, the cooking tops and even the furnishings can be made of natural fibers from coconut palms, Kirei or bamboo. These fibers are attached under pressure with formaldehyde-free glues.

ECO-VILLE

Architect: **OMD — Office of Mobile Design**
Completion: **2002 (design)**
Category: **residential and office**
Location: **Los Angeles, U.S.A.**
Construction materials: **translucent polycarbonate sheets, Kirei board, amber vertical strand bamboo, and coconut palm flooring. The structure is a steel modular moment frame**
Surface area: **1,506 sq. ft. (house), 500 sq. ft. (garden), 2 hectares (residential complex)**

Renderings © OMD – Office of Mobile Design

which Jennifer Siegal and her company chose as the design for the ECO-Ville, demonstrating that individual, modern solutions for homes are also possible using industrial manufacturing technology.

INSTALLATIONS CENTER II

Pich-Aguilera Arquitectos

The building is located in Santa María Benquerencia, to the east of Toledo city center: it is an area which combines homes and industry and is one of the most populated neighborhoods in the city. The building was originally constructed to provide services for different companies and businesses in Toledo, although since its inauguration it has been rented to the company Telefónica as a client services center for the subsidiary Telefónica Móviles,

and so the building is also known as the 'call center'.
The client was Gicaman (*Gestión de Infraestructuras de Castilla-La Mancha*), a public company belonging to the Industrial Department of the local autonomous Castilla-La Mancha government. This institution promotes all kind of public projects from sports facilities to theatres or social centers.
The featured scheme was to renovate an old warehouse. At the

time of the design and the execution of the work, there was no legislation in Spain governing sustainable construction. The new *Código de Edificación* (Building Code), which included this concept, came into effect in March 2006, after the project was completed.
The building, which uses wood as its main element, is a container of industrially manufactured elements, that are connected inside following the premises of bio-climatic control.

The structure is orientated towards the longitudinal north-south axis. The heating element is the glass roof which faces south to capture maximum sunlight during the day. The interior courtyard is located to the north and constitutes the cooling element.
The main spaces in the building are the rooms for telephone operators, the rest areas, offices, lecture rooms and meeting rooms.

INSTALLATIONS CENTER II

Architect: **Pich-Aguilera Arquitectos**
Completion: **2005**
Category: **commercial headquarters**
Location: **Toledo, Spain**
Construction materials: **wood, concrete, polycarbonate sheets, boards of recycled wood chipboard, ceramic shutters**
Cost (prefabrication): **3,500,000 Euros**
Construction time: **18 months**
Surface area: **49,514 sq. ft.**

Photo © Eduardo Sánchez López

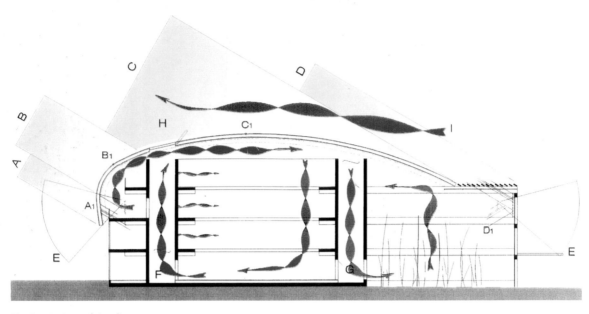

A   Direct gain from greenhouse effect
A1 Maximum percentage of sunlight penetration
B   Photovoltaic panels as partial sunshade
B1 Average percentage of sunlight which penetrates. Overheated space
C   Thermal collector (frequency of cylindrical bars)
C1 Minimum sunlight = sufficient illumination
D   Sunlight in illumination. North decks
D1 Reflection on north façade
E   Laminated wood panel (vision + reflection)
F/G Stratification columns
H   Natural ventilation cover
I   Low wind profile

Bio-climatic diagram (winter)

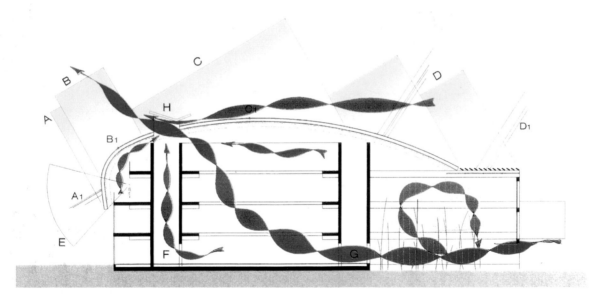

A   Direct gain from greenhouse effect
A1 Maximum reflection towards outside
B   Photovoltaic panels as partial parasol; overheated space. 'Buoy' effect of ventilation
B1 Average percentage of sunlight which enters
C   Thermal collector to feed absorption fridge (C1)
C1 Minimum sunlight = sufficient illumination
D   Deck overheating
D1 Reflection
E   Vision
F/G Stratification columns
H   Band of natural ventilation

Bio-climatic diagram (summer)

Given the high temperatures in this area in the summer, cross ventilation is very important. As heat builds up inside the building, more circulation of air is required to expel it.

The shape of the building and the general program are marked by the bio-climatic nature, which generates a plan of uses and functions so that each work-space has an adequate bio-climatic mechanism.

Other than their bio-climatic function, the interior courtyards are
designed as rest and relaxation areas. As it evaporates, the water
which is stored in the landscaped roofs of the courtyard on the north
façade cools the air current.

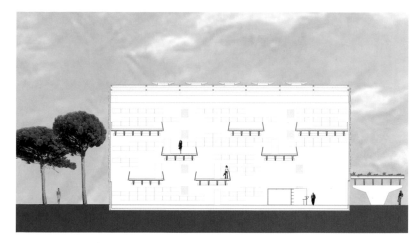

Longitudinal section

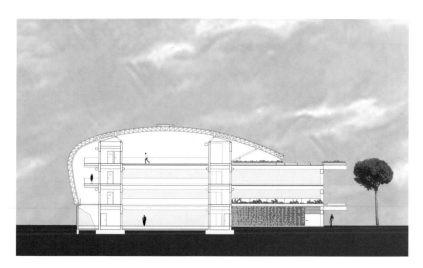

Transversal section

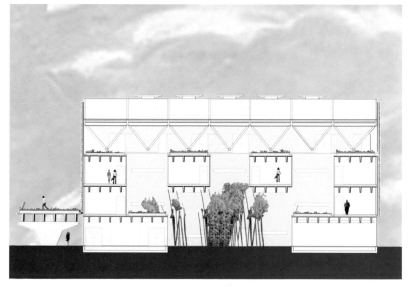

Section through courtyard

Solar panels make up part of the glass roof, which is the real bio-climatic motor of the building. The bio-climatic effect of the whole combination, which reduces the need for energy-expensive air compressors, is what the architects refer to as 'free-cooling'.

The call center is divided into three different areas:

1. The glazed façade which collects heat in winter. The heat accumulated is sent by forced ventilation to the deck on the north façade. This was intended to create a comfortable temperature in the area where the staff can rest and relax.

2. The glass roof works as the bio-climatic motor. Various mobile sections can be opened, creating a natural flow of ventilation inside the air-chamber of the double glazing. The transparency enables natural light into the building.

3. The atriums on the north side can also be operated mechanically according to the weather. In winter they are closed, receiving forced ventilation from the south side. To avoid overheating in summer, the solar panels are used to create shade, and cross ventilation is generated by opening the mechanism. This refrigeration process is accentuated by the evaporation of water in the hanging gardens there.

In the words of the architect: "During my analysis of the building I bore in mind concepts related to sustainability. Right from the start I knew the project would be very interesting from this point of view, but I have to admit that I was even more surprised during its execution: what surprised me most was the idea of completely industrialized construction." "I would like to comment that I fully appreciate the fact that the building's shape hasn't been a matter of impulsive aesthetics or formalism. Instead, this shape responds to the primary necessity of optimizing the sustainable features by means of orientation, solar incidence and internal air flows. The choice of the materials for their industrial character and high aesthetic values is also a fact I liked from the design process".

Euros. Telefónica Móviles currently has 500 employees working in the building, on different shifts throughout the week. The materials and the construction techniques were chosen, right from the design stage, to save time and money, and to prevent contamination.

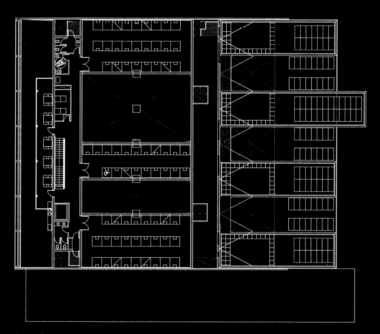

Fourth floor

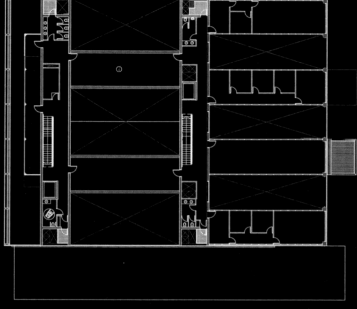

Third floor

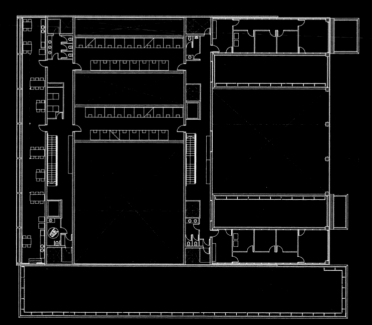

Second floor

First floor

0   3   6

VALLVERA SALT SCHOOL

Exe Arquitectura

This educational center is located in a rural area near the urban center of Salt, a city on the outskirts of Gerona, known for its high immigration rate. The client, GISA (*Gestió d'Infraestructures*), requested the construction of a complex for secondary education and training programs for students aged 12 to 18.

The main structure comprises three buildings, with the administrative departments on the first floor and the two upper storeys housing the classrooms and sports areas. The plan for the whole complex is a trapezium. The interior courtyards illuminate and ventilate the corridor on the first floor and soften the shape of the elevations clad in corrugated galvanized sheets. The construction system employed uses sandwich panels combined with perforated sheets to provide protection from the sun in the openings, and vertical, prefabricated concrete panels in the testers without openings.

The advantages of this system include the speed with which the project can be finished (essential, given the high demand for schools in this area), the ease of construction by using dry systems, improved safety during construction and better control of waste, materials and energy consumption during construction.

VALLVERA SALT SCHOOL

Architect: **Exe Arquitectura**
Completion: **2008**
Category: **educational installation**
Location: **Salt, Gerona, Spain**
Construction materials: **metallic structure, pre-tensed alveolar sheet, corrugated galvanized sheets**
Cost (prefabrication + installation): **4,300,000 Euros**
Construction time: **270 days**
Durability: **20 years (more with adequate maintenance)**
Surface area: **64,419 sq. ft.**

Photo © Lluís Sans

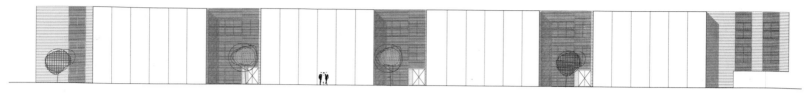

East elevation

West elevation

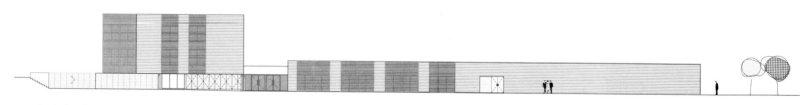

North elevation

South elevation

The use of corrugated galvanized sheets for the walls produces an
industrial style which harmonizes with the construction system used.
The simplicity of the shape makes the building stand out.

The similarity in the shape of some of the façades is interrupted by areas set back at equal distances, going up to the roof like internal courtyards. The west façade is more uniform and has cavities which serve as the entrance to the main building, as opposed to other openings which only have an esthetical purpose.

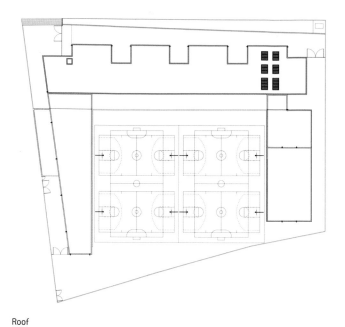

Roof

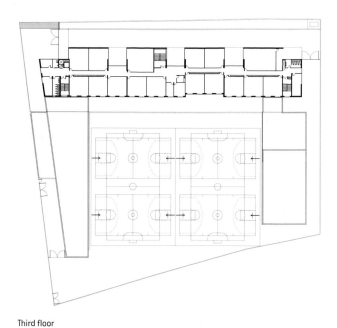

Third floor

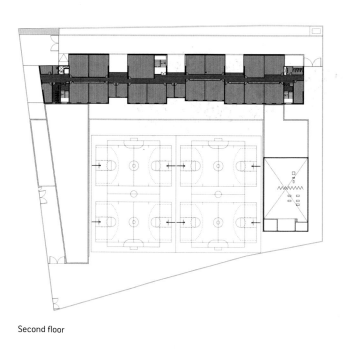

Second floor

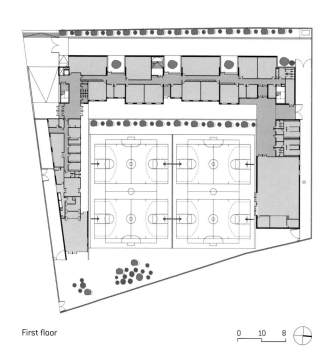

First floor

0   10   8

The complex includes a sports area with either four basketball courts or two indoor soccer courts.

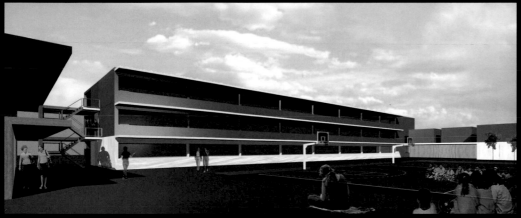

DIRECTORY

Alberto Mozó Leverington
Padre Letelier 0343
Providencia, Santiago, Chile
T. +56 2 494 1928
alberto@mozo.cl
www.albertomozo.com

Andrew Maynard Architects
Level 1/35 Little Bourke Street
Melbourne VIC 3000, Australia
T. +61 3 9654 2523
F. +61 3 8640 0439
info@andrewmaynard.com.au
www.andrewmaynard.com.au

Atelier Kempe Thill Architects & Planners
Vierhavensstraat 1
3029 BB Rotterdam, The Netherlands
T. +31 10 244 46 63
F. +31 10 425 47 23
info@atelierkempethill.com
www.atelierkempethill.com

Atelier Tekuto Co. Ltd.
Yasuhiro Yamashita, Junko Hirashita
301-6-15-16 Honkomagome
Bunkyo-ku, Tokyo 113-0021, Japan
T. +81 3 5940 2770
F. +81 3 5940 2780
info@tekuto.com
www.tekuto.com

Caramel Architekten ZT GmbH
Schottenfeldgasse 60/36
1070 Vienna, Austria
T. +43 1 596 3490
F. +43 1 596 3490 20
kha@caramel.at
www.caramel.at

DeMaria Design Associates
941 Manhattan Beach Blvd.
Manhattan Beach, CA 90266, USA
T. +1 310 802 1270
F. +1 310 802 1260
info@demariadesign.com
www.demariadesign.com

Despang Architekten
Lincoln Office
238 Architecture Hall West
Lincoln, NE 68588-0107, USA
T. +1 402 472 9956
F. +1 402 472 3806
Hannover Office
Am Graswege 5
30169 Hanover, Germany
T. +49 511 88 28 40
F. +49 511 88 79 85
info@despangarchitekten.de
www.despangarchitekten.de

[ecosistema urbano] arquitectos
Estanislao Figueras 6
28008 Madrid, Spain
T./F. +34 91 559 16 01
michael@ecosistemaurbano.com
www.ecosistemaurbano.com
www.ecosistemaurbano.org

Erin Moore
T. +1 520 400 2900
erin@floatarch.com

Exe Arquitectura
Llacuna 162, box 304
08018 Barcelona, Spain
T. +34 93 200 80 35
F. +34 93 209 36 92
marketing@exearquitectura.com
www.exearquitectura.com

Gerold Peham
Franz-Josef-Straße 3
5020 Salzburg, Austria
T. +43 662 876 016
F. +43 662 876 817
office@nomadhome.com
www.nomadhome.com

Holzbox ZT GmbH
Colingasse 3
6020 Innsbruck, Austria
T. +43 512 561 478-10
F. +43 512 561 478-55
mail@holzbox.at
www.holzbox.at

Korteknie Stuhlmacher Architecten
Postbus 25012
3001 HA Rotterdam, The Netherlands
T. +31 10 425 94 41
F. +31 10 466 51 55
mail@kortekniestuhlmacher.nl
www.kortekniestuhlmacher.nl

Neil M. Denari Architects Inc.
12615 Washington Blvd.
Los Angeles, CA 90066, USA
T. +1 310 390 3033
F. +1 310 390 9810
info@nmda-inc.com
www.nmda-inc.com

Olgga Architects
14 rue de l'Atlas
75019 Paris, France
T. +33 1 42 40 08 25
F. +33 1 42 40 08 59
contact@olgga.fr
www.olgga.fr

OMD – Office of Mobile Design
1725 Abbot Kinney Blvd.
Venice, CA 90291, USA
T. +1 310 439 1129, ext. 26
F. +1 310 745 0439
info@designmobile.com
www.designmobile.com

Oskar Leo Kaufmann & Albert Rüf ZT GmbH
Steinebach 3
6850 Dornbirn, Austria
T. +43 5572 394 969
F. +43 5572 394 969-20
office@olkruf.com
www.olkruf.com

Philippe Barriere Collective (PB+CO)
philippebarrierecollective@gmail.com
www.philippebarrierecollective.com

Pich-Aguilera Arquitectes
Àvila 138, 4-1
08018 Barcelona, Spain
T. +34 93 301 64 57
F. +34 93 412 52 23
info@picharchitects.com
www.picharchitects.com

RozO Architectes
2 rue Chapon
93300 Aubervilliers, France
T./F. +33 1 48 33 03 46
rozo.architect@wanadoo.fr
http://rozo.archi.free.fr

Scott Specht
1314 Rosewood Avenue, Suite 103
Austin, TX 78702, USA
T. +1 512 382 7938
F. +1 866 439 6908
zerohouse@gmail.com
www.zerohouse.net

SMC Alsop
41 Parkgate Road
SW11 4NP, London, United Kingdom
T. +44 20 7978 7878
F. +44 20 7978 7879
info@smcalsop.com
www.smcalsop.com

Stefan Eberstadt
Landsberger Straße 191
80687 Munich, Germany
T./F. +49 895 17 39 05 2
stefan.eberstadt@stefaneberstadt.de

Studio 804
1465 Jayhawk Blvd., Room 105
Lawrence, KS 66045, USA
T. +1 785 864 4024
F. +1 785 864 5393
rockhill@ku.edu
rockhill@sunflower.com
www.studio804.com

System Architects
124 West 30th Street, Studio 319
New York, NY 10001, USA
T. +1 212 625 0005
F. +1 800 796 4152
system@systemarchitects.com
www.systemarchitects.com